How to Publish a Book:

A Guide to Self-Publishing for First-Time Writers

Lauren Bingham

Contents

Introduction

When it comes to publishing books, there are generally two types of authors. The first searches for as much information as possible to carefully figure out a step-by-step process they can follow in order to set themselves up for the best possible success in their endeavors.

Then there is the type who thinks this introduction is already too long. This book falls somewhere in the middle, which I hope makes it generally accessible for both types of authors.

I personally fall into the "as much information as possible" category, which is why I will say honestly that this is not a book of specifics. I will not go into the specifics of the Big Five publishers. If you are looking for the magical formula that will instantly rocket your first manuscript to the top of the New York Times Best Sellers List, get you unending movie contracts, and set you on the path to superstardom, go ahead and put this book down.

But before you go, I need to tell you something very important. This is super-guarded industry information, and I might get banished to a purgatory where I'm only allowed to write in cursive with a crayon, but everyone needs to know this:

There's no magic, instantaneous way to get professionally published.

Yes, you can run down to the copy shop and print off a million copies of your manuscript, but you'd still need an ISBN and BISAC to properly distribute them. And you'd have to find a way to let a million people know that a copy of your book is ready for them to purchase and read. Once they purchase it, you'd have to get the copy to them, too. And honestly, at that point, you might as well self-publish it.

Hence, the book you are currently reading shouldn't be put down after all.

The path that one takes to get to international superstardom is the same path one takes to get their book into the hands of just one reader:

Step 1: Write "Book"

Step 2: Make "Book" very shiny and pretty

Step 3: Figure out how to get "Book" into the world

Step 4: Tell everyone about "Book"

Step 5: Profit!

If you're currently in the thick of your first manuscript, you probably won't believe me when I say that the first two steps are the easiest. You're likely eagerly looking forward to the day you bid farewell to your characters or wrap up your studious exploration of a nonfiction topic.

And yet, even though you may have typed the words "The End," your book is hardly done. That's where *this* book comes in handy.

Regardless of whether you have best-seller aspirations or just want to see what happens if you throw a book into the world, the steps to publication remain mostly the same. You've got to have an airtight manuscript that you believe in with your whole heart, and you have to have enough passion to make everyone else believe in it, too.

While this book is obviously centered on self-publishing your own book, we'll take a deeper dive into what the traditional publishing process looks like as well. We'll look at the resources you need to help you and where you can find them. I'll help you determine a general order of operations to help you figure out where you need to be and which of your talents you can use to help you follow the path in your own way.

You may wonder why I don't just tell you everything I personally did in order for your eyes to be reading these words at this moment. If I'm being completely honest (and why stop now?), not everything works just as well or even the same way every time. What I mean is that the Facebook author page that got you a ton of traction on one book may be as effective as screaming your book title into a ravine for the next. Your editor may miss a ton of silly typos that unwittingly thrust your book into "unreadable" territory. The book cover that you think visually expresses everything you tried to convey in text may be completely unremarkable compared to others in your genre.

So instead of giving you a specific set of detailed instructions to follow, I plan to give you some plain, heartfelt guidance to set you on the way towards discovering your self-publishing path. We'll cover terms you need to know—in case you're still puzzling over the ISBN and BISAC—and take a look at everything you need to accomplish before moving on to the next step. And fear not—there are resources at the end to help you find your way, even if you get a little lost.

The beauty of self-publishing is that, quite literally, anyone can do it. But before you cast your boat upon those seas for a solo voyage towards publication, I encourage you to take this three-hour tour through the basic steps to get an idea of what it really takes to self-publish in a way that makes the most of your time, effort, and money—and most of all, a way that honors your work as an author.

After all, it's *your* book!

Chapter One

A Very Basic View of the Self-Publishing Process

When I mentioned this book in my writing group, a friend joked that it should be released as an audiobook only, with actual recordings of the noises I make during each step of the process. It would start with chastising myself in disbelief as I scroll through page after page of obvious typos. That would be followed by a chapter of cursing under my breath when I find the very evident grammatical issues highlighted by my amazing editors. By the time we get to beta readers, it's mostly just a low, relentless creaking noise punctuated by moaning.

While this is a terrible idea, practically speaking, it does highlight two very significant things about the publishing process.

First, it is emotionally taxing. The process of writing your book was exhausting because you had to make yourself happy with the product. Publishing is draining because now you have to make other people happy with the product as well.

However, the second important thing about the publishing process is that resources and community are part of the package.

With this book, I hope to slowly walk you through the steps I mentioned in the introduction. We'll first take a look at the overall goals and activities involved in each step before we jump right into all the fussy bits that each step entails.

I don't intend to take on the role of your *only* lifeline to the writing community, so I'll share some resources to check out once you are ready to get the publishing process started. While not every voice you encounter will be kind or even helpful, I think it's important for every first-time publisher to know they aren't alone. Things are confusing, and things get messed up sometimes. But you know all about twists and turns—you're a writer! Even non-fiction writers get to drop a good surprise reveal from time to time, so consider us all in the same game together as we pursue the odd adventure that is publishing your first book.

Let's start with a slightly more serious approach to the steps of publishing your first book.

Step 1: Write a Book

It may seem obvious to write a book before you publish it, but technically speaking, you don't actually have to write a book in order to sell a book.

Readers who were around in the 1980s and 1990s might remember the glory days of real estate speculation. This is still very much a thing—people buy real estate with the hopes of turning a profit on future developments or the land itself. They seek investors and collect money before the deal is done. The investors simply have contracts in place—and faith that things will hopefully turn out in their favor.

But way back when, before the internet allowed us to access property ownership details or a satellite view of any location on the planet, unscrupulous people enjoyed quite a racket promising to turn a profit on properties that were owned by others or simply didn't exist. Swampland in Florida was a famous grift, but if it didn't exist, these cons would sell it. These folks made tons of money while the investors gained nothing but debt and a "trust no one" attitude going forward.

Likewise, you can technically jump into the book publication process at the third step and start selling a book that is just a mere concept. At the Big Five level, this is done all the time, as you'll soon see.

But for the purpose of your very first book, I strongly recommend having a fully completed manuscript on hand, or one that is at least very close to being fully completed. Regardless of the publishing method you choose, nothing delays a career more than waiting for that great idea that was so brilliantly marketed, turning out to be nothing like the proposed vision. For example, when I sat down to write, I thought I was heading towards a book on canine behavior. Instead, you are obviously reading a book that has nothing to do with dogs.

All joking aside, a lot of things can happen between your first concept and final draft. I have an entire folder filled with detailed book descriptions with relevant keywords. None of these books exist beyond those keyword-rich descriptions. Some just haven't shown up at the right time, while others were just outright terrible ideas that I somehow can't get rid of.

That is to say, don't put the cart before the horse. They say time is a construct, and it's even more of a boggling concept when you're trying to bring a book into the world. We'll look at timelines later to help illustrate this point in full, but for now, plan to have a readable manuscript in your hands/on your hard drive/in the Cloud early in the process. The "Soon" part of "Coming Soon" implies a short wait, so don't strain your audience's patience.

In fact, this is a great place to start considering everything you do from the perspective of your audience.

"Outrageous!" you might cry. "This is my book! The audience will take what I give them and cherish it always! I am the hero of modern writing!"

That may be true, but even Thoth made sure his audience of newly-literate Egyptian people understood what he was sharing with them. While we writers are stereotypically sullen, grumpy, and ferociously stubborn, your author persona is only part of the deal. Your book is a gift, yes, but your job is to make it a gift that people want to receive. That means stepping away from your role as the Passionate Creator of your text and becoming the Devoted Personal Assistant to your book's overall success.

In the next step, you'll be scrubbing, scouring, prepping, and polishing your manuscript so that it is fit for public consumption. If publishing is your goal, keep this fact in the back of your mind even as you prepare to write your book.

Step 2: Get Your Book Ready for Publishing

There are many editing programs available; in fact, you could write an entire book on your phone using Autocorrect. I cringe at how your fingers would feel afterwards, but that's aside from the point that it is very much possible.

That being said, how many absolutely glorious mishaps has Autocorrect given us? Most of us can name several situations that were made ten times worse by Autocorrect doing the opposite of what we want it to do. Turn "barking" into "baking" in an apology text, and suddenly the whole neighborhood wonders why your dog is making delicious treats and how they can get their hands on some.

Therefore, I encourage those who are serious about publication not to rely exclusively on editing software. Use it and use it well, but don't consider it your only source of grammatical guidance.

In fact, you may wish to enlist the assistance of an entire editorial crew. Much as Dorothy needed the Scarecrow, the Tin Man, and the Lion to help her reach Emerald City, you may need the assistance of several different people who each approach your manuscript with a new perspective.

The first crew you'll want to consider is your editing team. It is possible to get through the process with just one editor, depending on how many hats both you and your editor are willing and able to wear.

We'll take a deeper look at the various types of editors shortly, but for now, consider the following:

- Typographical errors

- Grammatical errors

- Factual errors

- Inappropriate/outdated references

- Terrible formatting

Ultimately, you want to keep all of these out of your book. And while you may correctly believe you can catch a lot of these, it takes a truly special person to catch all of them at once. In the highest levels of traditional publishing, each of these bullet points would receive its own editor, if not an entire editorial team.

Then there are the beta readers. Beta readers are individuals who read your manuscript before it's published. Where they join you in the process usually dictates their role. In the strictest sense, they're supposed to read your book and provide an overview of what works, what doesn't work, and provide a general review of how successful they feel your book is. If you're lucky, you'll encounter a beta reader who is kind enough to point out anything that might have slipped through the cracks in the editing stages. On the other hand, you may have the misfortune of hiring a beta reader who rewrites your entire book and still tells you it's terrible.

This is why many of us in the writing world recommend getting as many eyes on your book as possible during this stage. Everyone will have a different perspective; everyone will have unique feedback, and the more eyes that pass over the page, the more those pesky typos will make themselves evident. Just like weeds in a garden, some errors are invisible until someone points them out. And just as having a child point out a dandelion during the neighborhood garden competition might end your participation, having your readers point out simple typos can be devastating.

Then there's the matter of making your book look good. Whether or not you're supposed to, everyone judges a book by its cover. They also judge a book by its title, description, and search rankings when they try to find it online.

The very first step of marketing your book is deciding what it will look like. Regardless of whether you have illustrations in your book, you will need a cover that grabs the attention of your reader. It is entirely possible to publish a book without a full-color illustrated cover, but in order to self-publish, you will have to put something on the designated cover page. It would take a very niche reader to search for, purchase, read, enjoy, and provide a positive review for a book with a plain white cover. Not impossible, but again, my goal is to set you up for success. Therefore, we'll look at what it takes to make your book look just like you need it to look to survive the publishing process.

We'll also look at what you can do, what you should do, and what you should absolutely leave to the experts. While saving money is always good, sometimes we have to appreciate that professionals are called that for a reason.

Step 3: Select Your Publishing Path

Choosing to self-publish over traditional publishing is just the first step in your publishing path. There are many choices you'll make, regardless of the route you take, and while none of them are entirely "wrong" steps, they may not be as right for you as you anticipated them to be. This step is mainly about making the most informed choices you can and dedicating yourself to following them through.

You may have chosen this book because you're set on self-publishing, or you're ready to accept it as your only option for immediate gratification. Before you fully commit, we'll look at the pros and cons of self-publishing versus traditional publishing and how each process works.

If you're looking for a lifetime of wealth and notoriety, writing is a baffling yet respectable choice. Still, your best chances for this outcome lie in the traditional publishing route. It may take the rest of your life to get noticed, but once you've got that contract, you just have to sit back and let the words flow. Sort of. We'll get into the details more, but there are reasons why having your own personal literary team can be less than ideal.

If wealth and notoriety are less important to you than being able to hold, read, and smell your own book, then self-publishing is the way to go. This is doubly true if you want to have full control over your text, your manuscript, and your ideas. Self-publishing your book will give you the satisfaction of accomplishment if nothing else, and having the ability to personally take charge of you and your book's success means you're in charge of your own destiny. Again, I have to say, "sort of."

But there's more to it than that. Who will you have publish your book? What are the publisher's requirements? How much will it cost? Who prints the book and mails it to the people who buy it?

Or will you even offer the book in print? Some writers work strictly in digital e-books. Some offer audiobooks of their creations, while others stick to hardback and paperback copies. How will your audience read or interact with your book?

Before you spiral out into a world of questions you don't know how to ask yet, rest assured that we'll examine what's involved in each option and why you would want to pursue that avenue. Here's a small spoiler to keep you spiral-free: generally speaking, self-publishing makes the technical parts easy, and traditional publishing keeps most of the heavy decision-making out of your hands. Again, we'll worry about that more in another section.

Step 4: Market Your Book

I have no shame in admitting that this is my least favorite part of the publishing experience. You think you're good at Facebook and Instagram. You take marketing courses so you can be down with the lingo and up with the natural traffic. But your post was 2.2 nanoseconds too late for the one person who really needed to see it while they were mindlessly scrolling.

Marketing a book is a lifelong pursuit. The formula for marketing success is as follows:

[(Strong keywords + ad placement) x Absolutely amazing content] x (Time + Personal Strife) = Great Marketing Effort

But then you take that Great Marketing Effort and divide it by Luck^2.

This means that no matter how much studious care and deliberate analysis you do, the sheer fortune of Fate is still a big part of how lucrative your marketing efforts actually are.

That doesn't mean you shouldn't try, however.

In fact, that means that you should put forth your best efforts, draw up a budget that makes sense for you, figure out where your audience spends their time, meet them there, and do what makes the most sense for you and your book.

Since I'm divulging all of the secrets in this beginning section, I'll give you another one here: results generally come about slowly, but they're still results. Cherish every reader and find value in every critique, especially if you plan to write more than one book.

So yes, I've set up the expectation that marketing can be tricky, but I want you to know that it truly isn't impossible. It's also very much one of those situations where you should realistically look at what you *can* do with your time, your money, your skills, and the sheer amount of energy you honestly have to put into the process. Those values can each wax and wane over time, so I want to provide you with the information you need to understand the playing field. From there, you can decide what makes sense for you right now and come up with a strategy for what you might do in the future.

Once again, you'll have resources to help you. I encourage anyone who really wants to understand what works and why when it comes to the strange world of marketing to take an introductory course or online seminar about it. I've thrown in some links and educational resources to help you with this.

Another thing you'll want to consider here is your emotional resources. We'll review how to be realistic with goals so you don't have to fully sacrifice your life for the success of your book. Unless you want to, of course, but I don't recommend it. Wait for your third book, at least!

Step 5: Profit (Hopefully)

I'm guessing many of you have been sitting on one particular question since you ordered this book:

When do I get paid?

We can all deny it as much as we like, but when we put a book into the world, we not only love the accolades and validation that come with people telling us they love the book, but we also like eating and having a safe place to live, as well.

Whether or not you make it to millionaire status with your first manuscript depends heavily on the first four steps of this process. You have to have a decent book. It has to be tidy and ready to go. You have to choose the publishing methods that are right for you, and you have to market your book. None of these steps is negotiable.

What you do about it, how you go about it, and what you plan to get out of it are completely up in the air, however. They are also entirely in your control.

Before we get into the heart of this book, I'd like to set some time to answer a few questions. These are questions that help you identify where you're hoping to go with your first published book, and where you want to go with your writing career.

Obviously, plans change. Budgets get recalculated. Your favorite laptop decides to do this weird thing where the screen flashes, and even the repair expert can't diagnose it beyond "that's pretty annoying." But if you have some goals in mind, you have them in your grasp, however tenuous that grasp may seem at any given time.

Very, very few things in life come about in a strict linear path. Footraces, I imagine, baking, and scientific experiments are some of the few scenarios I can think of in which one really must follow the steps in a very specific order lest disaster occur.

You can take as long as you want to publish your book. Perhaps a joke with coworkers at your retirement party reminds you of a manuscript you put together in college—by all means, dig it out for publishing. You can edit it, not edit it, skip all the steps, or adhere to them with absolute precision. Once it's published, you can campaign your book as long and as hard as you wish, or not at all. That's the beauty of self-publishing—absolutely every facet of this process is in your hands.

Except for the luck part. I haven't had much success harnessing sheer luck, but when I do, rest assured, I'll write a book about it.

In the meantime, take a look at these questions, and think about how you would answer them right now. Again, these aren't final answers, and no one knows about them but you, so answer truthfully:

- What do you hope to accomplish by publishing your book?

- How will you know that your book is successful?

- Do you plan to make this a career or a hobby?

- How much time can you spend on your book each day or

week?

- What do you want to get out of your first book publishing experience?

- How will you recognize when you're trying too hard?

You're here because you want to publish a book. It's a fantastic feeling to search for yourself on Google and see links to your works. Holding your book in your hand for the first time is indescribable.

But in order to do this without losing your mind or your love of books, you've got to do it in a way that makes sense for you.

So let's start laying down some facts for you to start organizing and analyzing!

Chapter Two

Breaking Down the Process: Writing the Book

H ere is the absolute truth: If you think your book is good, it is good. But it is only good because you think it is good.

I'm not saying your book is actually terrible, and we've all been trying to figure out the right time to tell you. I'm simply pointing out the giant, pink, glittery disco ball of an elephant that hangs over any creative environment: taste is subjective.

I'm really sorry, but not everyone in the whole wide world will love your book. Your own family might not like your book. Your best friend may not even read your book.

But none of these mean your book is bad. It's simply evidence that everyone enjoys reading different things. We simply all have different perspectives, and the extra clauses that annoy one reader will be the magic hook that pulls in an entirely different type of reader.

So what does that mean for you as the writer?

In a nutshell, it means that you have a choice to write for the readers or write for yourself. This is not a strictly black and white situation, either.

If you are looking for your book to be easily marketable, sell a billion copies, and show those Big Five publishers that they don't know what they're missing, you might want to take a very deep interest in what the readers are saying. But if you want the sheer satisfaction of holding your book and don't necessarily give a whit if anyone besides yourself reads it, then by all means, do that.

Most first-time authors exist somewhere in the middle. While they'd love to be doing interviews on the morning talk shows and major magazines, they realistically will feel accomplished once they've got an ISBN (yes, we'll get to that), and everything else is icing.

If you're like many first-time authors thinking about self-publishing, you'd like to feel that the effort of writing a book was worth it. You know the process is going to be arduous and likely soul-sucking, but you also have this annoying glimmer of hope that keeps promising you, "If you write it, they will read." And if you identify with these statements thus far, it's highly likely that you're reading this book because you want to be as prepared as possible for the journey ahead of you, and you don't want to waste too much time or money fiddling around in the dark.

As mentioned earlier, the writing/publishing/creating/succeeding process is never linear. And as I'll continue mentioning for legal purposes, I don't have the magic recipe for success—just suggestions that have made the publishing process easier for myself and my cohorts in this weird world of writing. You may be able to accomplish each of these steps quickly and easily, and with full attention and dedication. You may not playfully ruffle the pages of your first volume for a few years. You may skip steps. You may modify steps to best fit your plans for your book.

What I provide here are merely suggestions based on my own observations. You can actually start the publishing process at any point in time—even as you write the book, or maybe 10 years later. Therefore, I encourage you to think of how these things can be adjusted to match your needs. Your book is already good—now let's make it everything you want it to be, whatever that is.

Identifying Your Audience and Niche

What is the last great book that you read? What did you love about it? Now think about the other people in your life. Would you recommend that book to a parent? Your teacher? Your child's teacher? A stranger, even?

On the other side of the coin, have you ever read a book someone recommended to you and wondered if they'd ever really met you?

The reason there are so many genres and subgenres of books is that they each have a different audience. There can be a lot of overlap in audiences, but it's not a guarantee. Take, for example, the entire *Star Wars* vs. *Star Trek* conflict. While I personally believe they're very different things and a person can like or dislike them equally, a number of fans declare a strict allegiance to one franchise over the other.

Therefore, it's not necessarily specific enough to consider your book a sci-fi adventure book. Is it about the pursuit of personal identity, community, and the meaning of "home" in a time of politically-charged wartime chaos, or is it about exploration, bringing cultural understanding to the universe, and mitigating politically-charged wartime chaos? Or is it about alien teenagers who go joy-riding in a rare Ferrari spaceship owned by one of the teens' fathers as a desperate attempt to capture meaning in a banal suburban alien life?

All of those are "sci-fi adventure" books at their core, but it's fair to say they're all quite different. Imagine if all the characters of these books were to meet—it's fair to say there would be some confusion and disagreement, along with a lengthy "getting to know you" period.

So, in order to figure out exactly what your book is, you'll want to pick out your audience.

Who Are You Writing For?

When posed with this question, many first-time authors will immediately report, "Myself." This is a glorious and noble answer, and I highly recommend it. I have several drafts that I have written exclusively for my own consumption. Because that's what "myself" means—that you are writing for the sheer satisfaction of watching your ideas appear in language. Absolutely do it sometime—the release is worth it.

However, if you plan on selling some, several, or many copies of your new book, you might want to amend your answer to, "Myself, and (genre)(demographic)(psychographic) readers who want to read about (topic)."

Let's go deeper:

Genre- This word refers to a category used to organize and classify creative works based on similar characteristics. A biography is a book about a person. A mystery involves a puzzling problem. Romance books involve characters developing intimate feelings for each other.

But it goes beyond that. You can have a tell-all unauthorized biography, an illustrated picture book biography for new readers, or a person's life presented exclusively in photos. There are murder mysteries, kidnappings, historical mysteries, supernatural mysteries, art heists, musings and theories regarding real-life mysteries, and cozy mysteries. I've seen romance novels in both Amish country stores and urban adult shops.

As you are conceptualizing your book, it's not a bad idea to narrow down your book's genre as much as possible. I say "as much as possible" because things can change significantly as you write, but as you're working, continue thinking of adjectives you would use to describe what you're writing. I typically think of words like "how to for beginners," "the writing process for newcomers," "when readers become writers," or "first-time creators." Not all of those are specifically genre or official categories, as we'll see later, but they help me recognize what the book is and where it's headed.

This helps me realize who I'm writing for. That, in turn, helps me recognize my audience. And the more I learn about the person who is reading my book, the better I can be at writing a book that they'll appreciate. The more appreciation they give, the more successful I feel.

<u>Demographic</u>- Literally, who is your audience? What is their age? How do they identify in terms of gender, race, or culture? Where do they live? What is their income? What is their religious experience? What type of socioeconomic status do they have? What level of education have they received? The last one is exceptionally important if you're writing children's books.

It's important to note that "demographic" does not mean "stereotype." Do not make assumptions; do your research.

That doesn't mean going door-to-door to ask potential readers what you should do. Instead, it means looking at what that population is reading, day in and day out (and not just books that are similar to yours!). What kind of things do they look for on Google? What kinds of articles are they interested in? We'll get more into how to evaluate what you find momentarily, but for now, take your time slipping into your target audience's metaphorical shoes.

Specifically, think of how they might encounter your book. Would your audience typically download your book from an online retailer for their e-reader, or might they pull it from a shelf and start gnawing on it with enthusiasm before their parents realized what their toddler had done?

Which brings us directly to the next point—what can your audience easily consume? New readers have a smaller vocabulary and shorter attention span. Readers who are middle-aged suburban stay-at-home moms may have a larger vocabulary, but an even shorter attention span due to the multitude of tasks they're juggling besides reading your book. Knowing what they can handle can help you adjust your book to make it easier for your audience to enjoy.

Psychographics- And then we get to the mind-reading part. Sort of.

Just as it is much more natural to have a conversation with someone who shares your interests and general opinions, it requires less effort to write a book for people who share your demographics. But think back to your classmates in school. You probably shared a lot of traits with them. You were all in the same age group, and you may have lived in the same neighborhood or gone to the same place of worship. In many communities, it's common to encounter your classmates outside school, whether you want to or not.

But did you really have that much in common with them?

While demographics allow you to pick your audience out of a crowd, psychographics are a method of understanding why someone would be drawn to your book. The study of psychographics includes gaining insight into how and why people hold certain attitudes and beliefs, along with their hobbies and life choices.

Does it matter whether your target audience votes a certain way, agrees with particular conspiracy theories, or recycles whenever possible? Maybe.

Demographics involves sorting people based on a few obvious common features. The study of psychographics puts that information to the side for a moment to group potential audience members based on what they like, want, and crave. Sometimes these things overlap. When they do, you're a step closer to identifying your target audience.

Again, you'll want to do your best to be a fly on the wall for your target audience. Why do they order their books online? Why do they use an e-reader instead of audiobooks? What makes them interested in your genre? What other types of things do they read? What's their fandom? How many different types of books do they read? What's their favorite music app, and what's on their most-played playlist?

At this point, you may be thinking I've just asked you to abandon all of your natural instinct, voice, and writing preferences, but that's not it at all. This is your book, and all of the choices are your own. However, the choices you make will directly correlate to how well-received your book is amongst its intended audience.

In order to communicate with any audience, you have to meet people where they are. You wouldn't want to write a teenage coming-of-age story in Latin, for example. Even if you know several teenagers who can read Latin fluently, it's not a huge market compared to readers who would be interested in a teenage coming-of-age story set in the Byzantine period and written in English rather than Latin, even though the characters would have used Latin frequently.

Your idea is a great idea, but at this stage, you don't want to focus too much on what a good book it is you're about to write. We already know that. Instead, consider this very important question:

What do you want readers to get out of your book?

What do you want it to mean to them? This is why psychographics matter. The hypothetical Byzantine teenager from the example above needs to go through some changes in order to fulfill the criteria of a coming-of-age story, so what kind of experiences would today's teenage readers be able to relate to? How would a modern teenager deal with your characters' challenges? Connecting the reader to the material is incredibly important in helping them enjoy their reading experience.

This is equally true of non-fiction books. If you're writing a biography of George Washington, what do you want your readers to get out of your biography? Are you going to focus on a particular section of his life to analyze and evaluate the choices he made as the leader of a brand-new nation? Are you going to focus on his truly peculiar death? Or are you going to spout a bunch of facts about the first President of the United States in a semi-connected fashion for the entertainment and enjoyment of the reader?

As you can imagine, each of those books would have a different audience. And while you don't want to lose sight of your own particular voice and the thoughts you wish to share with your readers, you do need to speak to them in a way that is familiar. Use the words that your reader would be familiar with. Create a tone that won't ostracize or bore them. Paint pictures in a way that will emphasize the details you want them to capture.

You can do none of these things, of course, and it won't change the fact that your book is still a good book. The difference is, a book written with the identity and understanding of the reader in mind gets more ratings and better reviews. You'll need to consider how important those factors are to you before you self-publish your book.

You'll also want to get a better feel for where you'll find your audience, and that means digging further into your chosen group of readers.

Evaluating the Market

This part is either very fun or completely arduous, depending on how much you love reading and how willing you are to put your ego on the shelf for a bit.

Go to a library. Figure out where your book would be on the shelves (I'd say "Use the Dewey Decimal System," but I'm not sure that's around anymore). Once you're staring at where your book would be, if it were already written, pick up all the books surrounding it and read them.

The first time I did this was in college. My writing advisor and mentor gave me a list of books I was supposed to read each week, despite the fact that I was already reading a ton of large, heavy books for my weekly classes. However, I was able to check out the short stories he recommended. And I felt the crushing weight of knowing I wasn't as good as Ray Carver, Alice Munro, or James Joyce.

But that's the point, isn't it? If every prospective writer gave up simply because there were better writers, no one would write. We would've chosen one writer as the Best Writer Ever—dare I say, the PEN-ultimate author?—and given up on anyone writing anything ever again.

So don't compare yourself to the people already on the shelves. They've already compared themselves to the people on the shelves before them and decided to write a book anyway. You can do the same.

Instead, think about what makes your book different. Even though they're about similar topics, the books that share the same library shelf are entirely different from each other. Yours will be different too.

As you're diving into books within your chosen genre, you may also want to scour the internet to see what other readers are saying about these books. What do they like? What kind of feedback do they share? You can look at reviews, book forums like Goodreads, or even social media discussions about these books.

Then go deeper. Find out everything you can about your chosen niche. Join book groups, online book discussion groups, or fan pages that your potential audience might also join. Learning what real readers love and don't love about books on your topic can help you avoid some of the areas your audience may find problematic.

Again, you'll find yourself wondering how to compromise your brilliant, original idea with what the readers are saying. And yet again, you'll need to decide how badly you want to be abundantly true to yourself versus establishing a meaningful connection with your audience.

This is why I encourage writers to focus on what sets their book apart from the competition. Maybe your authentic voice is the differentiating factor. Perhaps your ability to pluck the perfect descriptor from the ephemera is what makes your book outstanding on a crowded shelf. It could be your way of simplifying explanations or summarizing the boring parts, or a character that acts wildly out of the norm.

Once you've identified what makes your book different, think about how you'd like to use that information. Some authors lean so far into their particular quirk that it's really impossible to imitate them—Chuck Palahniuk comes to mind here. Others evaluate current trends and decide where they want to inject their own uniqueness in order to endear themselves to their prospective readers. Stephen King is particularly talented at this, as his writing blends current events and the author's opinions in an unmistakable voice.

While you're hovering in this stage, wondering what you should do with your ideas and whether pursuing publishing is still a good idea, I recommend creating a description of your book. It doesn't matter if your book is done yet or if you haven't even started.

What you're doing at this stage is committing to the task. Write a description in the format of the blurb you might find on a back cover, with full vigor: "In a world in which chaos rules, author Your Name brings order with *Your Book Title*." Or, for our non-fiction writers, "Those who have struggled to understand (your topic) will break through the fog with *Your Book Title* by Your Name."

Get pumped about it. Enthusiastically tell imaginary readers what they'll get out of your book. Paint your hero as you see them, and outline the learning points in such a way that everyone will understand how crucial they are.

At this stage, you're mostly selling your book to yourself. This is where you declare your book different from everything else in the world. These are your reminders to yourself that your book is going to be great. And to be perfectly honest, when I do this, about 80% of my earliest description makes it into the final blurb you might see when purchasing this book.

If you are feeling bold, consider sharing your early book description in writing forums or groups dedicated to self-publishing. You'll definitely get some feedback, and given the uninhibited nature of the internet, some of it might sting. Try to harvest constructive ideas from any criticism you receive, and remember that some people use the internet specifically to be as mean as possible.

Regardless of whether you share your book description at this point or not, you are now officially on your way to marketing your book, whether you realize it or not. Since we're still in the writing stage, it's important not to get swept away by these notions just yet. The full-on marketing part will come soon enough. This is the time to figure out how to best connect with your reader through your writing and the sheer existence of your book.

Another thing you can do at this point is get a feel for how your readers will prefer to enjoy your books. There are many options available today, including:

- Physical copies

- Audiobooks

- Online books

- E-readers

Which version does your proposed audience prefer? Furthermore, where do they get their material? Do they buy it? Do they borrow a copy from the library? Do they stumble upon it somewhere in the darkest shelves of the school book room? Do their parents receive it as a baby shower gift?

To find the answers to these questions, you'll need a handful of demographics, a few spoonfuls of psychographics, and a whole bunch of hunting and gathering, so to speak.

Information Gathering

While you are evaluating demographics and psychographics and be-coming enmeshed in the market you hope to join, you will likely discover some additional facts about your potential niche, if you pay very close attention to what folks are telling you.

For example, think about the process you'll use to help you get your finger on the pulse of your particular market. I've put a few potential sites in the Resources section, but I want you to search on your own, too. You'll discover that what you put into the search bar of Google (or whatever site you're using) can bring you many different results, depending on the words you use and their arrangement.

If I were trying to find the book you are currently reading, I might consider search terms like:

- How to self publish book

- Self-publishing for the first time how to book

- Book about publishing your own book

- How to book for self-publishing

- Non fiction book how to self publish

Now try it with your book. If you're writing a fiction book, you can go as far as you like. I've gone so far as to search for my characters' names to make sure I'm not duplicating someone else's efforts. The curious thing about search terms is that they don't necessarily have to make sense—in many cases, people word-spew into the search bar with no consideration for punctuation and syntax. "Book for teenagers parentified protagonist has a pet zebra dystopian science fiction" is better than nothing, and will likely start a search for something, even if you are the first person who has written a book in which a teenager with loads of siblings and little attention from her parents makes friends with the only zebra left on Earth after everything has been destroyed, and now she has to figure out how to get the zebra transported to the new planet without telling her parents. I'm hypothesizing here, or perhaps starting a new series. Only time will tell.

These search terms become what we call keywords when we're actively marketing our books. Keywords are words and phrases that help search functions find your book. You can use as many as you want, too, ranging from very broad ("how-to book") to very specific ("non-fiction how-to book about self-publishing author Lauren Bingham"). Typically, the more specific you get, the more likely it is that your book will be the first one that appears in the search results.

We like being at the top of the search results. We like that a lot, because people generally don't read past the first six search results. Rarely do they go past the first page of search results.

But we'll get more into keywords and what they do in the Marketing step. In fact, you'll be most prepared for the Marketing step if you do this type of information gathering, but I'll explain how that works at the appropriate time.

Use this time to search for your book, or where you would want your book to be once it's ready to be set free into the world. Pay very close attention to the results of each of your searches:

- What changes when you alter your search terms?

- What websites have appeared more than once in your searches?

- What types of reviews are these books getting?

• Where are people talking about these books (book reviews, literary groups, social media, Reddit, etc)?

Earlier, we used our internet searches to discover who was reading books in our genre, and what books they were not only reading, but enjoying. Now, we're looking more at how these individuals are finding these books, where they go to talk about them, and what terms they're using to describe these books when they're hunting for new material.

I strongly encourage you to take notes during your sessions. Jot down which searches seem more lucrative than others. Try to find books that are similar to yours. Try to find other authors in your genre. Find out which sites are easiest for accessing books that are just like yours will one day be. Use different sources and notice the differences in the results. Keep a list of potential keywords, because one day you'll be in the midst of your marketing strategy, struggling to remember whether that one search that was super helpful started with "non-fiction book" or "book non-fiction." These tiny differences may seem barely noticeable now, but they'll make a huge difference when you're actively promoting your book.

What other things do you notice about books in your genre? Are there any similarities in the covers? What colors do they use? What fonts are commonly used on the covers? What words are used in the official book description? You might start to notice keywords there as well, and as we'll discuss shortly, this is a very good place to put them.

Most of us are still in the "writing the book" stage at this point, so you don't need to do a full market analysis at this point. Just start making observations and taking notes. If all of the dystopian zebra friend books currently on the market have covers that are in shades of blue and have titles with words like "Friend" and "Lonely" in them, do you want to do more of the same, or do you want to go with orange and words like "Friendly" and "Alone"?

The answer to that question can depend a lot on what's going on in your market right now. Have you ever noticed that different printings of books have different covers, even if they're from the same publisher? Trends change. The average modern reader is not as heavily into leather-bound, gold-leafed pages as they were centuries ago, when books were considered rare, prized possessions among the aristocracy.

Therefore, think carefully about whether you want to be one of the many results that appear in a "lonely teen zebra friend blue cover" search, or the top result in a search for "friendly zebra teen alone orange cover." Each scenario has its advantages and disadvantages, but ultimately, you'll decide which path is best for you. In fact, you're about to make a lot of decisions about a lot of different things.

Chapter Three

Breaking Down the Process: Getting Your Book Ready for Publication

I n the last step, you were still writing your book, but now it's complete. You've wrapped up all of the plotlines, summarized the content, and typed "The End."

Now your book is ready for publication, right?

Like I alluded to earlier: if only. The next three steps are crucial to helping your readers find and recognize that your book is as good as you dreamed it would be. You must:

- Have the best possible manuscript

- Not have illegal content

- Make it look good

On the surface, these seem like easily achievable tasks. Spell check didn't go off a whole lot when you were writing, so you've probably got all of the typos cleared up. You thought of everything yourself, so everything is legal, and you're not personally publishing the book in your garage, so the looking good part will probably be up to the printer, right?

If I were writing a "How to Self-Publish" book for grade schoolers, I would absolutely agree with you. Except for the part about personally publishing your book—my first efforts were hand-written and bound in scraps of wallpaper. But by completing the steps I've recommended to you, I've identified my audience for this book as adults with loads of ideas and maybe not so much time or confidence, so I'm going to go into more accurate detail. While there's something very charming about a hand-bound book, that's probably not the type of self-publishing you're leaning towards.

So, let's dive into each of these concepts further.

Have the Best Possible Manuscript

When I say "best possible," I'm not trying to insult your manuscript. I really meant it when I said your book is good. Your concepts are unique, your treatment of the subject is inspired, and you've successfully committed a large number of sequential words to a digital medium to share with others. Manuscript accomplished.

Please note that I say "digital medium" because regardless of whether you work in Word, Google, or another file-sharing-editing software, your manuscript must be on a cloud or a drive or some place other than handwritten in a notebook in order to move forward. I know many individuals who like to start their drafts by hand—sometimes it does actually feel a bit like the automatic writing technique practiced by Spiritualists when you're first dipping into your new book—but you can't publish it like that. Not yet, at least. So you will need to type it up, or let someone else type it up for you if that skill isn't in your wheelhouse.

Not only will a typed, digital manuscript make it easier to submit to publishers and publishing software, but it will also make it easier to share your book with your team.

Who is on your team? Your team can consist of any number of folks who are interested in helping your book succeed. This might include an army of editors, a battery of beta readers, and at least one person with a solid sense of formatting. Let's look at each role in more detail.

Editors

When we think of an editor, our mind typically conjures up a person who reads through our manuscript and fixes all of our mistakes, grammatical and typographical alike. But there are many types of editors available to writers at different stages of their manuscripts:

- A Developmental Editor acts as a sort of live coach for writers, helping them understand and apply best practices as well as keeping them motivated.

- Copy Editors are the precise masters of the word world. They focus on each of the words you use to make sure it's used correctly and in the correct context. This goes beyond spelling and grammar, however, as copy editors also review your manuscript for continuity errors, inconsistencies, and my personal favorite sin, repetition.

- Fact-checkers are an obvious choice for those writing non-fiction books to ensure you're not publishing incorrect information. They're also helpful for fiction writers, especially if you're using a specific historical timeframe or location, or have characters engage in an activity in which you are not confidently proficient. What may seem like a minor detail for you might actually be a huge detachment from reality for those who are intimately aware of these times, places, and activities.

- Sensitivity Editing is done to ensure that the completed manuscript isn't offensive, but it goes a lot deeper than pointing out things that might not be received well by a specific audience. In fiction books, sensitivity editors can point out any character portrayals or dialogue that seem inappropriate, along with noting any character traits, actions, or descriptions that might not be accurate. They can also help with eliminating bias and inflammatory language in non-fiction books—especially if you didn't realize you said something wrong in the first place!

Many editing professionals wear multiple hats at once. In fact, it would be against the Editor's Code not to point out each typo or spelling error encountered, regardless of why they're supposed to be reading your book. Therefore, it's important to consider what you want your editors to accomplish and hire candidates who are able to provide those reviews.

Folks who have never used an editor before often fret that someone they don't know will "rip their book to shreds." Yes, this is the exact purpose of an editor; however, I encourage you to change how you think about it. They aren't ridiculing your failings as a writer—they're exposing the ways in which your book could be even stronger. That is, if they're a good editor.

I encourage you to always audition your editors, because some of them simply won't be on the same page as you—quite literally. If you ask your editor to focus on a few specific areas, but they can't get past the first paragraph because it isn't how they would have written it, that editor might not be the best choice for you.

You want your editor to recognize and match your stride and your style. Some editors are eager to rewrite everything in their own style, and admittedly, some editing agencies pay their staff by the number of corrections they make, regardless of whether those corrections were really necessary. In many cases, rearranging the words in a sentence or moving a few paragraphs around will make your manuscript much clearer, and you'll stare at your editor's improvements with tears of admiration welling in your eyes. In just as many cases, you'll wonder why someone has gone through the trouble of coming up with a synonym for every word in your sentence. I once had a copy editor decide they didn't like an entire chapter, so they removed it and wrote a new chapter on a completely different topic. It was baffling.

The process of auditioning an editor is fairly straightforward:

- Find an editor

- Send them a sample of your work

- Review their edits

- Discuss your thoughts about their edits

- Discuss their thoughts about your thoughts

- Come to an agreement about both of your thoughts, and either

    ○ hire them or

    ○ wish them well and say goodbye

Where do you find an editor? Many self-publishers choose free-lance editors because there tend to be more budget-friendly options among freelancers. That being said, never assume that a freelancer is free. In fact, for every college student, side hustler, or new-to-the-field candidate you find, you may find twice as many highly experienced, top-notch professionals who prefer the freedom of choosing their own clients. Consider your project and your budget fully before you start auditioning options.

When you're reviewing their edits, I encourage you to know what you're looking for. Are there any trends in things that they're constantly changing, and you aren't sure why? Do they leave comments and suggestions to explain what they're doing? How involved do they seem with your sample? Furthermore, when they return their edits, do they ask any questions, provide a summary of their efforts, or provide feedback?

It's true that the more you want from your editor, the more you must be willing to both pay and communicate with them. However, along that same line, the more genuine effort you receive from your editor, the stronger your finished manuscript should be.

Beta Readers

I actually got my start as a beta reader many years ago, so I have a very soft spot for these team members. I believe beta readers are a crucial part of the process because they are the first "real people" who will read your book.

The job of a beta reader is to make sure the book is readable and to provide genuine, unbiased feedback about the book. They can also point out any lingering typographical, spelling, or grammatical errors after you and your editors have gone line-blind from looking at the same manuscript every day.

That being said, it is not the beta reader's primary job to point out typos, grammatical errors, or other obvious accidents. They should certainly mention them if they find them, but having a long list of corrections means things have gone sadly awry during the editing process. Instead, you want a beta reader to share their overall impressions of the book, what they liked, any constructive criticism they might have, and who they feel might best enjoy the book. Essentially, your beta readers are the first audience to review your book.

If your book is a huge booger on the face of literacy, your beta readers will point it out, but they should also let you know why they didn't enjoy it and what you might want to do to clean it up.

If, instead, your book is reasonably enjoyable, they'll let you know what they want more of and what could be stronger to make it even more wonderful.

And, of course, if they tell you your book is "perfect; no notes," they didn't actually read it.

As with editors, you can ask your beta readers to focus on certain aspects of your book or answer particular questions. Did they see the plot twist coming? Do they feel the main character is likeable? Do they think your exploration of modern neuroscience is applicable to the intended audience?

Beta readers can often be found on freelancing job boards, as well as in writing forums, both online and off. You may also wish to bribe your inner circle of friends and family to serve as beta readers. Though their opinions may not be professional caliber, they do represent the reactions of the folks who might encounter your book in the wild. Personally, I feel the more eyes on my books, the better.

What should you expect from beta readers? A genuine opinion. I've received very angry feedback from beta readers who couldn't get past the first page because they hate my tone. Some beta readers love that I include a Resources section, while others write impassioned treatises about why that's a waste of everyone's time.

You will learn from your beta readers that there is absolutely no correct way to write a book. You will see firsthand that there is no such thing as a universally loved book. The lesson here is not to take this feedback personally, but to use it to fine-tune your book for its intended audience.

As with editing, you are under no obligation to accept all of your beta readers' feedback. Sometimes you'll get feedback like "I hate the main character's name." Unless every single beta reader agrees, that's just someone's personal bias, and you can safely ignore it.

On the other hand, if you get consistent feedback like "I don't understand the continuity between Point A and Point B" or "the main character's name changed three times," you should address that.

Generally speaking, beta readers aren't leaving line-by-line critiques like editors do. You generally won't get as many comments through the draft of the manuscript itself, but rather a full review following their reading. An adequate beta reader provides their impressions of the text, highlights things they liked, and provides specific areas that they found troublesome. They may also suggest some things you could do to help them enjoy the text more.

Carefully weigh the merit of each comment they make. Your beta readers will make suggestions, but it's up to you to decide whether

these ideas truly make your book stronger in the long run, or just
something that one intrepid individual would enjoy more.

In fact, that brings us to the final step of making adjustments following the editing and beta reading stages. You've got opinions by the
fistful, so now what should you do?

How Do You Decide What Advice to Follow?

Have you ever visited a restaurant, had a mind-blowingly amazing
experience, and decided to leave a positive review, only to discover
that others have absolutely blasted that place with negative feedback?
Chances are high that you read further to discover some of those
1-star reviews are things that are kind of tertiary to the experience,
such as "They have terrible napkins. I'll never return" or "I promised
my kid a grilled cheese, but they said they don't have that because
this is a drive-thru coffee shop that doesn't serve any food – horrible
service." You can usually tell which reviews were left by folks who
were inconvenienced by reality or maybe didn't fully interact with the
establishment as intended.

The same is true for the feedback provided by your editors and beta
readers. I remember getting one manuscript back in which exactly
4/25ths of the readers actually understood what was going on in the
story. If you picked up on all of the clues left throughout the text,
you'd slowly realize you were reading a psychologically dark story.
Unfortunately, I had not considered that some readers wouldn't pick
up on the clues, so they just read a bunch of stream-of-consciousness
ranting. In that particular instance, I conceded that I am not William
Faulkner and ended up rewriting some of the stream-of-consciousness
ranting bits so that it told a story, as well.

This sounds incredibly simplistic, but once you've received all of your edits and beta comments, you'll have to decide where to point your book in order to give it the best chance at your definition of success. That might mean rewrites, that might mean clicking "accept all changes," or that might mean starting over with editors or betas who understand your style more.

Regardless, don't rush the process. Let your editors and beta readers take their time. Encourage them to leave detailed feedback. Ask them questions and let them ask you questions. And above all, pay them adequately!

Formatters and Designers

Regardless of whether your book has pictures or not, it is a fantastic idea to hire someone to take a look at your book to make sure it will look good. After all, an illegible book is really hard to sell. Some editors are also very good at formatting, and they will help you put your book into a recognizable format in addition to plucking out the errors and kindly escorting your text to greatness.

There are many different types of formatting out there, including APA, MLA, AMA, Turabian, and Chicago, to name a few. Mainly, these refer to citations and referencing other authors and pieces within your text, but there are certain layout rules associated with each, such as spacing, indentation, font, page numbers, and a table of contents.

In the 1990s, when I received the bulk of my education, we had the Chicago format drilled into us. As someone who received both Theatre and English Writing degrees and learned how to type on an electric typewriter, I reflexively tab, capitalize, and ellipsis according to my training.

But according to all of the formatters and editors I've worked with (and deeply appreciate), that's wrong. We don't do Chicago anymore. Some prefer APA, and others are into MLA. Some want all of the text center-justified and double-spaced, while others feel that's a sin. Sometimes, watching multiple readers go back and forth over the formatting in my manuscripts is like watching the scene in the Disney version of Sleeping Beauty, in which the fairies argue over what color to make Aurora's dress while their cottage nearly explodes in bright flashes of proposed colors as notes and messages of different colors pop up on my screen.

However, neither the editors nor you as the author have the final say on this—the publishing software does. When you load your book onto whichever self-publishing platform you choose (we'll get to that momentarily), it has to fit into whatever rules have been set into that software. So, the formatting you started with in your original manuscript may look very funky once the publishing software gets hold of it.

This is where the formatting or designing expert comes in. Traditionally, "formatting" refers to making sure the words fit the page, and there aren't any huge incongruities in how the text appears on the page. Outside of the writing world, few readers will notice major shifts in format unless you start indenting all willy-nilly. However, they will likely get grumpy if you keep shifting between bullet points and numerical lists, or if some of your paragraphs lean against each other. A formatting expert goes line-by-line through your text via the publishing software to make sure it is spotless and easy for your audience to read.

A designer, on the other hand, usually has a more complicated role. Books with tables, charts, and graphs can benefit from a designer, as can those with pictures or photographs. Those of you who are writing children's books and want to be extra-conscious of how words appear on a page may also wish to work with a designer to ensure you're not chopping up the text.

Sometimes, you'll need input from both types of roles. Poetry, for example, may not have pictures or tables associated with it, but the shape and spacing of poetry are often integral to the reader's experience. For textbook-style works, those with loads of external references, and books with appendices or bibliographies may need the opinion of both professionals.

You may even find talented individuals who are happy to perform both types of tasks. Come up with a scope of all the things you want your format or design expert to accomplish. Ask them for their portfolios, or perhaps a small sample of previous work, so that you can get an idea of their experience. This is especially important if you're working on a book with lots of visuals. Look for things like continuity across the pages in spacing and formatting. Are there any errors? Is spacing even in all places? Do things line up the way you expect them to? Most self-publishing platforms allow you to see a preview of your text before it's live to readers, so make sure things don't just look good in the software—take a detailed look at any previews or pre-runs to make sure they fulfill your dream.

Artwork

There are some instances in which worrying about artwork makes sense. The aforementioned picture books, photographs, charts, graphs, and tables—all of these things will clearly need to be created if you plan to include them in your book.

There are a few situations, however, when your book might be improved with a little artwork. Perhaps a photo or two in a historical book or biography will provide a visual example of the subject matter. Fiction readers of all ages typically don't complain if they get a complimentary image or two, either. If your characters have a treasure map, blueprint, or family tree that is important to the plot, you might want to throw that visual in as well, rather than trying to explain it:

John walked down the hallway, which had two red doors to John's right and three green doors to the left. After these doors, the hallway made a weird bend in which the right wall had a 45-degree turn, while the obtuse angle on the left made about 160 degrees. The stairwell was on the left wall after the bed, which John was technically sort of facing. It was off-putting and made John dizzy.

Yes, and it makes the reader dizzy, too. It may be very well worth the investment to add a little artwork to keep everyone focused on the plot.

But what if you're planning on writing a book like this one? Or maybe you've got a tasty little fiction number up your sleeve, but you weren't planning on adding illustrations.

Why would you need to consider artwork in these cases?

Because your cover is going to sell your book, of course! Everyone judges a book by its cover, and even if your book never exists in print format, you'll still need some kind of page providing the title and the author's name. In theory, that page doesn't need to look special, but in practice, things with a little visual pizazz usually gain more attention than those that are more plain.

There are very skilled artists, photographers, and designers who specialize in book covers and illustrations. Many times, they specialize in a certain genre or niche. For example, an illustrator may work specifically on early picture books, or a photographer will focus on frogs. They do this for a very simple reason: they're good at that style of art and feel confident they can provide you with what you need at the price you can pay. It is generally a waste of everyone's time and money to attempt to persuade an artist to work outside of their style... unless you are offering them a very lengthy amount of time and an obscene amount of money.

Even then, you've got to find the right person for the task—so how do you know? I recommend scouring portfolios. Again, you'll find your candidate pool on freelancing job boards. You might also look around in your community for folks who do artistic things as a side hustle. Regardless, look at many examples of their work before you hire them.

You'll also want to know exactly what you want before you hire an artist. What data is included in your charts and graphs? What photos do you need to tell your story or explain your topic? What does your main character look like?

Your artist may make suggestions to you, but they won't spontaneously create perfect artwork for you. Have an idea of how many illustrations you need, what size you need them to be, and where you want to put them. Give them an idea of the subject matter and what goals you're attempting to accomplish with the visuals. Encourage them to read the manuscript, or at least provide them with a synopsis that helps them understand how their work will be incorporated into yours.

You'll want an artist you can collaborate with, who will help you create what you need. If they become defensive at your questions or refuse to make paid revisions, you might want to find a new artist.

At the same time, remember how hard you worked during the editing and beta reading phases of your book to make changes based on someone else's opinion. While you should get what you've paid for in the end, give your visual specialist some room to work in their own style. Come up with actionable feedback, such as "I want a portrait of my main character on a stormy day," rather than "I don't like the blue." No matter how much you and your artist jive on a personal level, neither of you is actually a mind reader (in most cases), so use specific words to explain your thoughts, and provide critiques that give the artist direction in how they can make your dreams come true.

Special Considerations for Audio Books

While you're musing over what your book needs to achieve excellence, there's an aspect of audiobooks that we haven't mentioned yet: the actual audio recording of someone reading the book.

You can, in theory, rig a microphone up to your laptop, download some audio recording software, and make it happen. However, I caution you with the same advice I gave in the section about things you can do for yourself: you get what you pay for.

If you are an established voice actor with a fantastic recording gig, then you've already paid your dues in reaching this point in your career. But, if you're like most of us—prone to clearing your throat, sniffing, or stumbling over words after a few pages—it might be worth the investment to hire a professional.

Hiring a voice actor is much like hiring any other team member, in that you've got to find the right one for your book. You may wish to review several samples from different individuals to get a feel for which candidate best connects with your book.

If you've written a fiction book, consider how the actor reads each of the characters and the narrative. Do they have different voices for each character? Do they seem to connect with characters, or do they need a lot of direction on how the dialogue should be delivered?

While some non-fiction books aren't suited for audiobook format due to technical formatting, too many visuals, or technical directions that can't be followed by listeners behind the wheel of a moving motor vehicle, many non-fiction authors have nevertheless found success with the audiobook format. In particular, "How to" books, lifestyle coaching, memoirs/biographies/autobiographies, and history books can make great "reads" for the right person. If you choose to release your non-fiction book as an audiobook, you'll want to make sure the voice actor narrating the text doesn't lapse into a dry monotone. Instead, you'll want to choose a candidate who understands the material and why someone would be excited about it, page after page, minute after minute.

You'll want a contract for your voice actor as well. Know what your goals are, understand what you're looking for, establish a timeline, make sure you're both using the right file type and software for the publication platform you've chosen, and agree on a pricing structure ahead of time.

Ergo, one of the limitations for releasing your book as an audiobook might be the cost of hiring the right person to make it happen. You may wish to hold off on releasing an audio version of your book to make sure this is the right format before you invest in quality audio recording equipment and talent.

Make Sure It's Legal

Raise your right hand and repeat after me: *We do not plagiarize.*

We just don't. If you want to use a quote from another writer to help support your non-fiction text, or to add to the emotional context of your fictional work, you can. You just need to appropriately credit it. This circles back to the citations we talked about earlier.

There are many different ways to cite source material, depending on the format you choose, how many citations are required, and why you're incorporating others' work.

For example, if you're doing a quick, one-off quote, you can often get away with providing full credit within the sentence, such as:

As Tyler drove away from his mom's house, he thought about what Bobby McFerrin sang in his 1988 hit song, "Don't worry; be happy."

But if you're really going in deep with the reference, you might want to be more studious about giving credit:

As Tyler drove away from his mom's house, he thought about what Dr. McFerrin et al published in their 1988 study of phosphatase inhibitors, in which they reviewed the effects of... (and so forth).

In this second example, you would want to footnote and create a section of the book in which you provide adequate citation of the materials quoted or referenced. That typically includes the author or authors of the material, the title, where it was published, and when it was published, but the exact order and details depend on the formatting you choose to use. Fear not—there are examples in the Resources section to get you started on the quest of learning how to properly cite your own sources.

But what about fiction books? Can you name your space hero Luke Skywalker and get away with it? Probably not. Most of the really big names are fully licensed and protected. There are exceptions, such as parody, but you'll still need to go to extreme lengths to ensure the person who invented that character doesn't pursue legal action against you.

What does that entail? Personally, I haven't borrowed a character since I wrote some *Bunnicula* fanfic in the 1980s. However, that would still be technically illegal if my 7-year-old self had actually tried to sell my wallpaper-bound copies. It's the part where you try to make money off of a character, location, and written words that causes problems.

How deep does the infraction go? For example, what if you write about an orphan in space who's about to make an amazing discovery about his true history? Is that copyright infringement? No, but it's coming a little close. If said space orphan is being raised by his aunt and uncle, who have a moisture farm and pick up two android friends right before intergalactic chaos breaks out, you've flown too close to the sun, and lawyers might be calling you. Many books share similar themes, and that's fine. You just can't borrow so much that it's recognizably not yours.

If the copyright has expired, however, you have the ability to borrow a bit more. The phrase "public domain" refers to work that is no longer copyrighted, never was copyrighted, or has been donated to public use by the creator.

There are legal considerations with your cover and artwork, as well. Publishing other people's photos—both photos that others took and photos in which other people are the subject matter—can be tricky business. If you're using photographs, make sure you're allowed to use them. If you're not sure what that entails in your state or country, I've got a few links in the Resources section, but I strongly encourage you to meet with a lawyer who deals in copyright materials for the specifics of your individual query.

You'll also want to avoid using material that belongs to other people—modern Disney characters, in particular, come to mind. They are very recognizable and can be quite helpful in selling your book, but Disney keeps a tight leash on its licensing. That's why you'll see so many Markey Mouse and Daniel Duck knock-offs trying to elicit a buck or two through familiarity. The exception here is the Mickey Mouse seen in the 1928 short "Steamboat Willie." That exact visage, and no other, is public domain. The one with the clubhouse and a bunch of friends? Off limits. The one in the wizard's robes? Hands off! See how tricky it can be?

To stay on the safe side of the law, I always encourage new writers to be as original as they can be. If you're not sure, do a quick Google search for your characters' names, just to make sure your villain isn't actually a hero in another part of the world. There are editors who also provide copyright checks on your material, along with plagiarism-detecting programs on the internet that can help you figure out why that particular phrase sounds so familiar.

I encourage all prospective published authors to take a look at the United States Copyright website for specific details. Most likely, many of you now have a few questions about your own work, and there are so many if/then statements involved that we don't quite have the space to cover all possibilities.

Unless you're writing a particularly inflammatory piece of non-fiction, you'll likely get a sternly worded letter asking you to knock off any copyright encroachment you may inadvertently commit. However, if you have a lot of facts, photos, or references to real people, you may also wish to hire an editor who specifically focuses on the legalities of your book and all material in it. Fact-checkers often provide this service; you may wish to ask any prospective candidates whether they can check citations and borrowed text to make sure you've borrowed it correctly.

What Can You Do Yourself?

Technically speaking, you could do your own editing, beta reading, and design work. There are plenty of editing programs available that can scan your manuscript and provide suggestions. Some self-publishing sites have software that makes it incredibly easy to upload your file. You may be incredibly talented at drawing, too, with a functioning awareness of how to load your designs.

I encourage anyone who is writing a book to get some kind of editing program that scans their documents for errors and makes suggestions for improving clumsy grammar. But it won't take the place of a human's opinions about your voice and tone.

It's pretty much essential that every author read their book after they've finished it to make sure it actually turned out according to plan (more or less) and isn't useless drivel. But that won't help you understand what other readers like and don't like about your book.

If you are confident in your photography, drawing, or chart-making skills, feel free to apply them here. I might encourage you to find a second pair of eyes to look at your final version, though, because there's no pain like the cringe of seeing a typo in a caption or graph axis.

Saving money is both noble and necessary, but you don't have to spend a ton of money to get more eyes on your book. My earliest attempts were read by anyone who would pause long enough to browse a chapter. My friends, my coworkers, friends of friends, and even one of my clients provided their opinions and thoughts. I bribed them with whatever they craved, including but not limited to Diet Coke, lunch at a local Mexican restaurant, and watching their dogs when they went on vacation.

Yes, you want well-educated eyes on your book to help you create the most powerful, honest, and successful version of your vision. Yes, you will need to pay professionals money in order for them to do their job. Therefore, it's important to figure out what kind of budget you have.

I encourage you to start shopping for editors, beta readers, designers, and artists as you're working on your book. Sometimes you'll find
gold in the strangest places—a friend's daughter once received extra
credit in her English class for beta reading my book. She made fantastic
suggestions, too, since I hadn't originally considered the manuscript
from a teenager's perspective.

I've made a few suggestions for hiring a freelancer for each of the
roles we've discussed. Take a look at any available prior work, and
consider offering a short sample of your work to get their impressions. Make sure you feel comfortable communicating with the final
contenders. Discuss in detail all expected timelines, deadlines, and
payments throughout the process.

Don't agree to their pricing structure if you can't pay their expected rate. I recommend using digital payment methods that track
everything you send to your team rather than the old "spreadsheet
and check" method. Some freelancing sites have their own payment
vehicle, but even familiar sites like PayPal and Venmo have options for
tracking payments to your team members.

Share all of your expectations up front—it's important that you
let your candidates determine if you're a good fit as well. Don't be
shocked if a prospective team member turns down your proposal for
editing, beta reading, or design. The stars need to align somewhat
to find an individual who is comfortable working with a new writer,
who has a style that meshes with yours, who understands your goals,
communicates openly with you, and is capable of meeting all of your
deadlines. If someone shares that they aren't in alignment with the
scope of your project, that's not a bad thing—it gives both of you the
opportunity to move on to another option that might be a better fit.

I recommend establishing a contract with anyone you hire for
monetary payment. If your cousin was going to read your manuscript

for 4 bean burritos, but they forgot, it's annoying. If the person you hired for several hundred dollars forgot your manuscript, there are potential legal ramifications. Keep yourself covered by writing a list of expectations for both your team members and yourself, sign it, and have the other party sign it—there are eSignature programs that allow you to fill out and retain contracts between you and your team members. This contract can include:

- What will they do/overall goals?

- How will they achieve them?

- Details regarding all milestones and deadlines, including the procedure in case these dates change

- The amount of payment, when, and how it will be distributed

Even if you're not sure whether or not you're comfortable being the boss and having other people look at your book, I encourage you to write out a sample contract. You might discover your goals are a little more specific than you originally thought. That's ok—every client and every editor is different. Just make sure you remain true to your goals, and don't change the game while your team is trying to work.

Early in my career, I worked for a lot of writers who wanted more personal validation than help stumbling through grammar. They often withheld payment if my review included any recommendations, suggestions, or changes. That meant that, unless I provided a glowing, ego-stroking review of their book, I didn't get paid for my hours of careful reading and consideration. It was a lot easier to just not take the jobs that required this service and select jobs where I would get paid for my honesty and skill.

The same can be true of artists and designers, as well. I've worked with artists who didn't want to read my book and designers who wanted to argue with the publication platform requirements. Neither was a pleasant experience. When you're establishing your goals with these team members, include provisions for edits, additions, or changes. Talk to your team members to determine what constitutes a simple change and what would be a complete redesign—and what each of these services would cost. Encourage them to communicate any questions, thoughts, or comments they have about the assignment as well.

Remember, you want honest feedback. Not all of it will be in your favor. Criticism should always be constructive, but that doesn't mean it might not be hurtful or totally counter to how you're approaching your manuscript. No matter how many of their suggestions you actually implement, if your team members have accomplished the goals you agreed upon, they have done their job properly.

After all of the tears and sweat you've put into writing a book, you may not be eager to have others provide their feedback about your literary "baby." Writing a book isn't exactly a relaxing hobby, and you may not be mentally or emotionally prepared to receive critique right away. In that case, you might want to wait a bit before submitting your manuscript to others' opinions. I encourage you to be brave, however. Though I've gotten some almost laughably abrasive feedback in my career, nearly all of it has taught me something very important not only about my prospective readers but about myself as a writer.

Chapter Four

Select Your Publishing Path

The purpose of this book is to provide new writers with guidance along the self-publishing path. But before you commit fully to publishing your book on your own, you'll want to make sure it's the best fit for your long-term goals.

It is certainly within the realm of possibility that a self-published book could get discovered by a major publishing house and become a *New York Times* Best Seller that inspires both a blockbuster movie and a Tony Award-winning musical. It's possible. It's not likely, but it's not impossible, either.

Instead, the books that make it big time are typically those that are represented through the traditional publishing path. The steps you've completed thus far—Writing a Book and Making It Good—are necessary regardless of which path you choose. But before you fully commit to the future of your book, let's take a look at what sets self-publishing apart from the traditional publishing path—and why you might want to choose one over the other.

The Traditional Publishing Path

If you are not excited about hearing the phrase "No, thanks," you may not want to pursue the traditional publishing path. Most of my colleagues who have chosen this path will have the door slammed in their faces several hundred times before anyone decides their book might be worth a second glance.

Therefore, it is extremely important that your book be of the highest grade before you start the process of trying to sell it. Yes, you will get fancy editors once your book is accepted, but you have to get to that point first. Generally speaking, publishing houses aren't looking for a fixer-upper—they're looking for a writer who can help them make money, quickly.

The process for traditional publishing is remarkably straightforward in concept:

1.**Carefully consider and determine the right genre and category for your work.** You might be thinking, "I already did that," and if you've been following my guidance, you did, because I encouraged you to do that early in the process. Some authors do not, and that makes the first two steps of this process a bit harder.

2.**Search for agents or publishers who are likely to appreciate your work.** Agents and publishing houses are looking for particular material to sell to their specific clients. As a result, you'll find agents usually specialize in a specific type of writing, such as memoirs, children's non-fiction, historical fiction, or faerie romance. Choosing to send your work to an agent or publisher that doesn't work with that genre is more or less a waste of your time and hope.

Much like the last step, this will be much less strenuous if you've done the recommended pre-work and have a good idea of what's going on in your intended market.

3.Create an appropriate submission. Generally speaking, no one has time to read your entire book in one go, especially not extremely busy professionals who are constantly inundated with requests. Beginner picture books might be the exception to this, but overall, you want to submit concise information that demonstrates your skills to a prospective agent. You want to give them the "Old Razzle-Dazzle," as they say. Carefully read each submission guideline to determine what they're looking for. We'll come back to this part in a second.

4.Submit your stuff, wait for a response. Again, make sure you've submitted all of the things requested—no more and no less. Many things are done digitally these days, and you have to make it past the front door by doing exactly what is asked. Otherwise, you risk a bunch of keyword-sniffing, attachment-detecting bots turning you away and declining your submission without even reading it. If the agent asks for an email with links, send just that—no attachments.

You may not feel you're doing enough, but remember: they know where to find you if they have questions. Do not follow up with them to elicit a response, either. The saying "Don't call us; we'll call you" is in full effect here.

For the most part, this may seem pretty direct. Find the right names; send the right stuff. One could say that being an Egyptologist is straightforward, too: Dig the right holes; find the right tomb. But just as there are uncountable handfuls of dirt and sand in Egypt, the number of competitors you might have at any given time is astounding.

Let's start our own deeper dig into the process of getting noticed in the traditional publishing world.

How to Query Agents and Publishers

First things first—should you look for an agent, or go directly to the publishing house?

Both are valid options, but the truth is that around 75-80% of the books that come through major publishing houses are sold to them via agents. Agents play a much bigger role in the publishing industry than you might expect. They have contacts throughout the industry to help them network with the most appropriate publishing house and even an editing team dedicated to the success of your book. They have their fingers on the pulse of the book world– they know what everyone is reading, where they're buying it, and what they're saying about your niche. They also help coordinate contract details between you and the publishing house to ensure you are paid adequately and that your rights and ownership of your work are protected.

Your agent will also request a cut of what you make, usually around 15-20% commission on everything you get paid. A less scrupulous agent may try to get as much money out of you as possible, so keep in mind that additional agent fees aren't currently common in the literary world, at least not as of this publishing. Be cautious of agents who try to milk you out of your entire budget, especially if they make wild promises about your financial future.

Ultimately, you want to connect with an agent who is trustworthy, communicates clearly, acts in your best interest, and wants your career to flourish. This may seem like a bare minimum, but overeager authors often settle for less, subscribing to big promises for big bucks.

While there will be more information in the Resources section, one very popular outlet for new writers to start their search for an agent is Publishers Marketplace. Please note this is not an endorsement or indicative of a partnership with this site—it's just one site where major international publishing houses go to post jobs, and where independent writers like you can go to break into the literary world. Currently, Manuscript Wish List, Query Tracker, and Poets & Writers' Literary Agents Database are also relevant sites for agent shopping.

Do a lot of searching on this site or whichever agent/publisher job site you choose. Look at other writers, publishers, agents, even the "Other" category, if applicable. Understand the community. Find your niche. Much like the first day of school, this is a bit overwhelming and scary, because you don't know where you're going to find a new friend. Unlike the first day of school, this is all done digitally with a Search feature, so you don't actually have to make awkward conversation right away.

I encourage you to browse many listings, paying close attention to information like client lists or publishers with whom the agent regularly works. Have they published work similar to your book? How well have those books been received, both critically and in sales? Also—make sure any prospective agent is a member of the AALA—the Association of American Literary Agents. Publishers generally prefer working with agents with established credentials.

Carefully read their listings, as well, and check out any links they may share. Do you feel comfortable with the idea of working with this person for a long time? Does their wording make you feel confident and inspired, or somewhat intimidated by how they might respond to your contact?

By the time you reach out to anyone on Publishers Marketplace (or a similar site- again, we're not affiliated), you should feel confident that you can start a conversation with them, because they will have told you exactly how to do so.

Some common requests in a first submission include:

- **Query letter**- Much like the cover letter you might send to a prospective employer, this is a one-page document that succinctly summarizes you and your work, with most of the focus on your work. This is essentially a sales pitch, but try to be genuine. Communicate in a way that feels natural, because you just might end up with a 5-book deal and have to work with this person every day to ensure you get paid.

- **Synopsis**- Most commonly used for works of fiction, this is a one or two-page summary of your book, including the ending. This is why I recommended writing a synopsis earlier in the process, and why I encourage you to finish your first book before you start querying agents. They need to know how your book ends in order to know if you're marketable. If you don't know how it ends or the ending might change, wait until you know before contacting agents.

- **Proposal**- There really isn't a proper definition for what is included in a proposal. Typically, you'll include an outline or proposed Table of Contents, a synopsis of the entire book, and a sample chapter or two, but it's important to pay attention to the details in the request. In his book *On Writing: A Memoir of the Craft*, Stephen King notes that he once received a rejection for using a staple instead of a paper clip. Agents can be that picky because they're trying to mainline your success. If you take their requests seriously, they'll take yours just as earnestly.

- **Samples**- Generally speaking, you'll only want to send a single chapter as a sample. It's good form to send the first chapter, but ultimately, you want to select a chapter that makes it easy for a reader to drop in and understand what's going on, regardless of whether your book is fiction or nonfiction in nature.

So what happens when you land an agent?

Mostly, you continue waiting. Your agent will get busy trying to sell your book. Ostensibly, they'll want to do this as quickly as possible so they can get paid, but anyone who's tried to sell so much as a picnic table on Facebook can tell you that it's about finding the right buyer at the right time. And even when you do, things might not proceed as rapidly as you might expect.

Getting Paid: Understanding Advances and Royalties

You might be wondering when we get to the part with the great big fat paychecks. Hopefully, that part should come relatively quickly once your agent has found a buyer for your book.

The publishing house that buys your book will likely have some notes about your book, with ideas that they feel will make it "stronger." Again, this means "more marketable." Based on how well the publisher believes your book will perform, the contract they offer you will include an advance and royalties.

The full term is really "advance against future royalties." For your first book, you'll likely get an advance amount in the low thousands (speaking in 2025 US Dollar terms). This will be paid to you in installments as you work on the final copy of the book. You're paid in advance of the book being published.

However, it's important to note that you will not receive royalties until your book has sold enough copies to recover your advance. Your advance is the amount of sales your publisher is confident they'll sell. Your royalties are for everything earned after your book has paid back the publisher. Royalties are generally paid as a percentage of the publisher's net revenue—that is, any profit your publisher makes on your book is split with you. You then split your profit with your agent.

Then you do it all over again for your second book.

To understand how this plays out, let's use some basic numbers:

Congratulations! Your agent sold your first book! The publisher has given you an advance of $1,000. They'll pay you $100 each week for 10 weeks until the book is done. Yay!

Now your book has been published. In the first week, it sold 800 copies. In the second week, it sold 1,000 copies. Then it was spotted in a celebrity's handbag, and it sold 10,200 copies. How much do you make?

Royalties are often paid based on the type of book sold—paperback, hardback, or eBook, for example. Rates often range from 4-8% for paperbacks and 10-15% for hardback books. Some eBook rates range up into the 20% area.

The total copies sold in this scenario equal 12,000. Let's say 6,000 of them are hardback books paid at the 10% rate, and 6,000 are paperback books paid at the 5% rate, just to make the math easy.

But wait—you're not getting 10% of every hardback book sale. You're getting 10% of what the publisher makes from those 6,000 hardback books.

In this example, let's say each hardback retails for $20, so that's $12,000 total from selling those 6,000 books. Then, of course, you don't start earning royalties until your book has grossed over $1,000 in sales. After that, your publisher needs to pay your editor, the designers, the person who did the cover, any assistants that were involved in the process, and then there's the matter of how much marketing costs. Once all of that is subtracted from the gross profit from your book, we've got the publisher's net profit. You get 10% of that, and your agent gets 15% of that. Still a hearty paycheck, but not enough to quit your day job.

Your publishing company will handle most of the marketing and making your book known to the masses. You may be asked to do readings, appear at conferences, give interviews, or participate in other activities to help promote your book. That doesn't necessarily mean you'll be on the national morning news shows right off the bat, but you may be asked to pop in at a local bookstore or library. Your publisher will want to take every opportunity to put your book in front of an audience that just might buy it.

When a publisher offers you a contract, read it thoroughly. Most big publishing houses have lengthy, detailed contracts that outline what they expect from you and what rights you'll retain to your book. For the most part, marketing and publicity for your book will be out of your hands, and if the publisher spins the story so that your least favorite character is now the hero, chances are good they did so within the terms of the contract. You can, of course, reject the contract, but remember, it might be a long time before you sell another manuscript.

The Other Path: Self-Publishing

So let's get back to the path where you don't have to face years of rejection: self-publishing.

We've already discussed the path one takes to get to the point of self-publishing, so let's get to the details of what happens once you've finished and polished up the book.

1. Choose your publishing platform

2. Select methods of distribution (hardback, paperback, eBook, audiobook, etc)

3. Decide how much your book will cost

4. Obtain ISBN and BISAC

5. Upload your book and illustrations

And just like that, you'll have a book. Unlike the traditional publishing path, which requires waiting for someone to want to buy your book, this process takes just as long as you make it take. That is, you could easily tick off all of these steps in a day, if you wanted. But let's dig a little deeper to determine if that's really the case.

So Many Choices

The first three steps should actually be one big step, because a lot of the decisions you make about platform, methods of distribution, and pricing will depend on the other two factors in the trifecta.

But to simplify and organize each individual activity, let's start by researching the various publishing platforms available. It is impossible for me to exaggerate how many options there are for you to choose from. Amazon KDP, IngramSpark, Draft2Digital, Apple Books, Kobo, Lulu, Smashwords, Barnes & Noble Press... This is just a sampling of options that come from a simple Google search for self-publishing companies.

While each of these companies provides your ultimate goal of allowing you to self-publish your book, there are some differences be-

tween what services they provide—some of which are pretty important. Therefore, I encourage you to take a detailed look at each one.

As you do, ask yourself:

- **How will I distribute my book?** Some of these sites
  will not only publish your book but also allow you to use
  their platform for distribution. That means people who hear
  about your book will hop onto a website, order your book,
  and the site will take care of sending it to them. Other sites
  distribute published books to specific retail sources. Still
  others allow for eBook publishing only. If you choose a
  self-publishing site that doesn't handle sales for you, you'll
  still need a way for people to request, pay for, and receive your
  book, which may mean frequent trips to the local Post Office
  or a very busy email address.

- **How will I earn money from my book?** Self-publishing sites that handle distribution have unique methods for
  handling payment—specifically, how much you can charge,
  what you'll make off of your own book, and how frequently
  you can receive that payment. If you're selling your book
  yourself, you'll need a way for people to pay you, as well.

- **How easy is it to use this platform?** What is the process
  for uploading your book and all associated artwork? I mentioned before that some printing platforms have their own
  software that you'll need to contend with—is it easy for you
  to use that software, or are you watching online tutorials
  with a quizzical expression, wondering what language the
  presenters are using? While every program has its "quirks"
  (looking at you, Excel), it shouldn't require Herculean effort
  to upload your book, and any associated help tools should

actually be helpful.

As you can see, choosing which platform you use to self-publish your book also involves knowing how people will be consuming your book. As mentioned, some self-publishing platforms offer services only for eBooks. If you're dreaming of signing the cover page of your novel for a long line of adoring crowds, eBook-only won't grant your wishes.

Those who are "publishing" audiobooks have multiple choices as well, but again, you'll want to pay close attention to where your book can or will be distributed, and how. Many music streaming platforms include access to audiobooks. How will you get paid when someone downloads or listens to your book?

Knowing how you want to distribute your book can impact where you publish it. At the same time, knowing where you want to publish your book can also influence how you distribute your book. If you know that most of your readership is going to want an eBook, but your dear sweet Nan wants an audiobook, perhaps you publish your book through a site well-known by your niche, and make dear sweet Nan her own personal recording. In other words, don't pay for services that can't possibly issue a return on your investment (more on that shortly).

So, which is best: print, eBook, or audiobook? You may even be wondering why you shouldn't do them all.

When tumbling down rabbit holes chasing demographics and psychographics, I mentioned that you ought to keep an eye on not just who reads your books, but how they read your books. Readers are often happy to share their favorite method of delivery in regular conversation. "I listened to (book) on my drive home from work every day, and when I got to (sordid part), I almost drove off the road!"

Furthermore, avid readers are almost always ready to debate which
is the best way to absorb the contents of a book, though there are a few
points we can mostly agree upon:

- Physical books feel and smell amazing, but their size and
  shape can be limited

- eBooks are great because you can store a full library on a
  device you can carry just about anywhere

- Audiobooks are a great companion for long drives or doing
  chores

Connecting with real readers in your niche will help you gain insight into what their particular opinions are on this matter; in fact, it
can be as simple as asking about preferences in a Reddit or Facebook
post.

Now you've got to connect with real readers at a more important
point: their wallet.

Pricing Strategy

In theory, you could make enough money from sales of your book
to balance what you've spent on it. You could actually turn a profit.
Better, you might be able to make enough off of your books that you
have a handy side-hustle running in the background for fun money.
You could even make writing your entire career.

However, any earning potential is based on how you price your
book. As you make decisions about how you'll issue your book and
through which service, don't forget about the financial considerations
on both sides of the table. You know how much you've spent to bring

your book into reality, but you might not know how much readers are willing to spend for the privilege of having their own copy.

During the pre-publishing stages, I encouraged you to figure out who is in your niche, what they're writing, where they're selling it, and how they're selling it. You'll also want to pay attention to how much they're selling it for.

Sometimes this depends on the publication or distribution plat-form you select. Some allow you to change the prices frequently so you can run sales or "specials" on your book. Some have a set fee per book published, so you'll likely want to charge your customers more than whatever that fee is. Paying close attention to price and payment details on the distribution site you choose can help you avoid any problems in collecting your hard-earned money from your customers.

Regardless of which platform or method you select, you don't want to price yourself out of your segment. If everyone else's download costs $1 and your book costs $4, it's unlikely you'll get the traction you want as a new author. However, if everyone else is charging $1 and you charge half of that, you might get a few more readers. As your reputation builds, you can work your way up to charging the same amount as your competitors, but don't be too anxious. Intrepid readers will read just about anything for little to no investment, but even die-hard bibliophiles will be reluctant to spend a ton of money on an author or book they know nothing about. We'll talk about pricing more in the marketing stage, as well.

Numbers and Codes

Amidst all of this decision-making is a task that is much more straight-forward and pleasantly low-risk. Obtaining your ISBN and BISAC doesn't really involve much rumination at all.

Your ISBN is your International Standard Book Number. Much like the product code you would find on anything you buy, the ISBN is a number associated with a barcode that appears at the end of every book intended for commercial distribution. The handwritten book with a wallpaper cover does not need an ISBN. Your eBook about making wallpaper covers, sold on Amazon, does need an ISBN.

You will need to purchase one ISBN for each version of your book. Your paperback book will need its own ISBN. Your eBook will need its own ISBN. Everything gets an ISBN.

The official ISBN Agency for publishers in the US and its territories is Bowker, which I've added to the Resources section for you. In order to obtain ISBNs for your book, you'll set up an account with Bowker and purchase ISBNs directly. You'll then need to follow the instructions provided for assigning ISBNs to each title/version of your book.

Remember, this number is international, meaning you are free to distribute your book around the globe. It verifies that you are the owner and publisher of the written material attached, thus making it more difficult for others to plagiarize your work.

"BISAC" is an acronym for Book Industry Standards and Communications. The BISAC Subject Codes List is considered the US Standard for retail books. The BISAC helps determine where your book lives on both digital and physical bookstores.

You will want to choose three codes for your BISAC to help accurately identify it. The fantastic news is that BISAC codes cost nothing. You don't need permission to use them, and you can look up the entire BISAC Subject Headings List online, for free. Unlike an ISBN, which provides an international, recognizable serial number for your creative property, a BISAC is a categorization that will help others find and enjoy your book, much like putting a label on your bookshelves at home.

The code is the most specific way to identify your book, and it will be used to categorize your book for distribution. You might choose a code like "Fiction" or "Juvenile Nonfiction" as the first code.

There are also subheadings under each code. Juvenile Nonfiction can be classified as *JNF001000 JUVENILE NONFICTION / Activity Books / General* and *JNF003370 JUVENILE NONFICTION / Animals / Worms*, depending on the angle you've taken.

That being said, you shouldn't start choosing random codes all willy-nilly. This is a method by which readers will be able to find your book among all of the other self-published books in the world. Be honest and thorough when choosing your codes.

Now that you've decided where and how you're going to publish your book with the necessary numbers and codes to sell it for a price that makes sense, it's time to do just that.

Most self-publishing platforms claim to have user-friendly publishing software. They don't necessarily specify to which user that camaraderie is directed. But it's never too late to hire a designer or formatter to help you with your piece. There are individuals who primarily help with formatting on publishing platforms, which can be especially helpful when something rage-inducing happens, like your linebreaks getting lost in transition, making your manuscript one continuous block of text. While most of the time this goes off without a hitch, it's always important to check everything to make sure it looks exactly right before you publish it, regardless of who put it there.

Once your book goes live via the self-publishing platform, that's it. You've published a book! No one has necessarily purchased it yet, but you can officially say you've published a book. Now you need to do everything you can to help it sell the way you want it to sell.

The Pros and Cons of Traditional Publishing vs. Self-Publishing

Reading through the past two sections, you probably saw some things you liked and didn't like about both methods. Truthfully, there are many things to like and dislike about each process.

To help you decide, consider this more condensed version of the pros and cons of each option.

Traditional Publishing

Pros

- Generally provides a higher profit faster, thanks to advances

- You have an entire team of editors, designers, artists, voice actors, copyright and formatting experts

- Your marketing and social media will be handled by a professional hired by the publishing company

- Your book will be available at major book retailers, seen by millions of readers

Cons

- Getting paid beyond your advance is based on how well your book sells

- You generally don't have any say over any of the changes or decisions made about your book

- You won't have control over most aspects of the publicity campaign and may not be able to independently market your book at all

- It may take many years and many hundreds of rejections for it to get there

Self-Publishing
Pros

- Instant gratification—you don't have to wait for someone to find your work profitable in order to publish it

- You have complete control over every creative aspect of your book

- You get to decide where, how, and to whom your book is advertised

- You can pick how you want to distribute your book and change it at any time

Cons

- In order to make money, you have to make sure the book sells well

- You may have to hire a team to help you get your book ready for publishing, which is money out of your pocket

- All marketing efforts are up to you; you've got to make some big decisions about how to spend your time and money

- You'll have to figure out how to send people physical or electronic copies of your book and payment details

It may seem like a black-and-white decision at first. Either you have no control over your book and loads of money (hopefully), or you have all the control over your book and you have to spend loads of money in order to make any money (probably).

Some people choose self-publishing because it is the "fastest" option. In terms of immediate gratification, yes, it is. You won't have to wait for the perfect buyer, and you won't have to sweat for months wondering what the editing team is doing to ensure your book is fit for consumption by the masses.

But if you have high aspirations for your book, you're going to have to appreciate that it may take some time for you to conjure up enough money to pay editors to take your book to a marketable level. You may have to save money before you can hire a photographer or artist. ISBNs aren't free, so you'll need to factor that into your budget as well. We'll talk a little more about time and cost expectations in the next section, but for now, I encourage you to be gracious with your timeline for achieving your self-publishing goals. It takes professional companies with all of the right employees years to turn your manuscript into a book, so don't make self-publishing a race. Instead, let it be a process that just takes a little less time than the traditional publishing route.

And even sweeter still, there's no one to tell you "no." If that sort of thing motivates you, that is.

There's nothing to say you can't try both, as well. Some authors have one manuscript on query with traditional publishers while they self-publish other volumes. Granted, that means you'll have to pop out more than one book, but I've got a helpful series of books to help you keep your head in the game, if you choose to go that route.

Personally, I enjoy self-publishing because of the freedom. Yes, the next step can get a little hectic, but like every other step, success is based on your own measurements. You don't have to pay back your advance, nor do you have to play politics or maneuver around another party's rules. I enjoy having dialogue with my team members via document comments or email, instead of having multiple meetings with multiple parties to smooth out the parts where I get a little nonsensical.

But would I also love to stand in front of an auditorium, doing a little read-aloud from my latest book? Absolutely. And I just might, someday.

Chapter Five

Selling Your Book

I t stands to reason that if you publish your own book, you have
to sell your book, as well. Sadly, there is no self-publishing fairy
who peruses new books to determine which ones should sell. Even
if there was, there's no guarantee that said fairy would work in your
favor, anyway.

If we want to sell copies of our books, we need to make people aware
of our books. Marketing is the process of advertising, promoting,
and otherwise bringing attention to our products – in this case, our
manuscripts.

The exact methods you use to market your book are going to be
unique to your particular publication. If I could simply read your
book and give you a distinct and definite recipe of how much of each
type of marketing you need to do in order to achieve success, I surely
would. And I would charge you for it, because there are plenty of
freelance marketing professionals who do exactly that. But we don't
need to jump to that level of marketing just yet.

Promoting your self-published book is something you can do slowly, over time, and with as much spare time and change as you have
at that particular moment. What I have provided here is a very brief

overview of some of the more popular things self-published authors do to market their books.

Don't start pushing your book until you're fully prepared. Carefully review the potential avenues I mention here and determine if they really make sense for your book—a book like *Intro to Advanced Astrophysics* will likely have a wildly different marketing path than *Baby's First Barnyard Sounds*. Then go for a deeper dig in the Resources section. Fall down a rabbit hole. Subscribe to marketing blogs. Take an online course or two.

You might be thinking, "But I'm just a writer. Why do I need to take marketing classes?" When you sign up to publish independently, you must also market independently.

If you have more urgent plans for your book, I strongly suggest hiring a marketing team or, at minimum, an analyst with a background in promoting books to help you get a good idea of where to put your advertising efforts and dollars to get the best return on investment (ROI). You will need to pay this person for their expertise, but it will take less time than learning to do this on your own. This part is all a matter of balancing time, money, and skill, so seriously consider each before you proceed.

Regardless of who is doing the actual marketing, I encourage you to keep reading this section to help you appreciate the scope of your role once your first book has been self-published.

In fact, it's fair to say that marketing your book truly begins with the title and cover art, but doesn't stop there, of course.

In your pre-publication research, you likely learned some of the most beloved books, television shows, video games, professional works, and adjacent publications in your projected niche. Don't use the same titles. That's just confusing and may violate someone else's copyright. Don't just rearrange the words, either, because that's not any better. In fact, it's often even more confusing.

Instead, your title should be unique. However, you can make use of a little thing called "keywords."

Keywords are important because of algorithms. But let's back up a bit so you can get an idea of why these things matter in the first place. Cookies track trends in your browsing history and online activity. These cookies essentially feed the algorithms, which is why the same ads follow you from site to site. When you search for things, these algorithms not only base the results on the best result for that search, but also the result that is most related to the things that interest you. On social media, you often see posts from people you regularly interact with rather than the folks you might scroll past or only occasionally "Like." All of these are examples of the algorithms at work.

Algorithms aren't inherently evil, as some may believe. Yes, they make things tricky, especially if you have a job that involves an intense amount of research, like mine does. Write one article about the Corvette ZR1, and suddenly my news feed, social media, and alerts are all centered around a very specific fast car. It's all because my browsing history included the ZR1 website and a lot of related terminology, like "Chevy ZR1," "fastest production Corvette," or "Corvette press media."

In the online world, that terminology becomes keywords. These are the words people use when they search for things online. There are both long-tail and short keywords. A short keyword would be something very general, like "cheese pizza." A long-tail keyword uses additional words to become even more specific, such as "vegan cheese pizza with gluten-free crust."

Including keywords whenever possible – the title, the blurb, any summary, even in the lines of your book—is one way to persuade the mysterious algorithm, creating search bots to pay more attention to your online presence.

Once you're published, you exist. When you're ready, you can let other people know you exist. And keywords are the crumbs from the cookies that lead the algorithm right to your newly published book. You just need to know where to put them.

It is possible to do too much. Any work that seems to have too many keywords or a nonsensical array of keywords may be flagged as spam, due to what's known as "keyword stuffing." Keep it natural, and you won't have to worry about anyone questioning the legitimacy of your work.

Marketing is the practice of understanding how this happens and using the tools available to you—which I will disclose here and in the Resources section—to help you use technology to your advantage. It is an art and a science, and I encourage you to invest in a few basic marketing classes to help you get a feel for the water before you jump in face first.

Read on for an overview of some of today's most common marketing concepts, along with how each outlet can be helpful for your overall book campaign.

Helping Readers Find Books in a Digital Age

Alright. So we've got the keywords, the cookies, the algorithms, and all these other terms buzzing around in our confused heads. Where do we start? What are our options?

There are many ways to announce your book. You can put up flyers at places where your readers might hang out. Advertising your dragon book at a Renaissance Festival, for example, is entirely appropriate.

You can print t-shirts with the main character's witty catchphrase. You could rent a billboard.

However, we ultimately live in a digital world; thus, digital marketing is typically a solid place to start promoting your new book. Make the flyer, wear the t-shirt, go wild with the billboard. Just make sure people can also find you online.

There are many different types of digital marketing, but some of the more popular among the self-published are:

1. Social Media

2. Websites and Landing Pages

3. Email Campaigns

4. Online Ads

5. Giveaways

Let's go deeper on each of these methods to help you gauge which options are right for you and your book.

Social Media

Chances are high that you or someone you know actively browses and engages with posts on social media sites such as Facebook, Reddit, Instagram, X (formerly Twitter), TikTok, LinkedIn, Pinterest, YouTube or some newer iteration of these sites. The massive reach of these platforms makes them very attractive for promoting your new book. That massive reach, however, is what makes marketing on these sites somewhat difficult.

The actual process of setting up a social media account for your book is fairly easy. When doing so, I encourage you to create either a professional user page for yourself or one specifically for the book. While you might get some traction from using your personal online handle to tout your title, you might not want anyone curious about your book to engage with your personal details. We all have That One Picture that's meaningful to our friends or family, but might raise a few questions when viewed by someone who doesn't have the context. Keep your business and private social media lives separate when trying to draw attention to your book and yourself as an author. This doesn't mean you have to fake it, either. It's not about pretending to be someone you aren't so much as it's about protecting yourself from anyone who doesn't have your best interest in mind.

Once your account is set up, you then need to figure out how to get people to follow you. There are many organic ways to do this, all of which take time. Use your book account to follow other accounts where you might find potential readers. Engage with other members. Don't make every conversation about your book, either. More people are likely to check out your book if they're interested in your thoughts as another person first.

You may recall that I encouraged you to start researching groups, forums, and pages related to your genre and niche before you even published your book. By keeping your eyes on what people are talking about before you've even finalized cover art, you've gotten a serious head start on marketing. You may have already interacted with your future readers by offering them support and suggestions. They may have returned the favor. Whatever interaction you've had, it's never too early to announce a project to those who might want to cheer you along (provided you actually follow up with a finished product).

In order to please the algorithm and help your page become more visible, you'll need to post frequently to each of your social media channels. These posts need to be unique, too, not just links to your sales site. The algorithm disregards sources that post the same thing over and over, with the understanding that these are frequently bots or spam pages. You have to prove that your page is run by humans by posting different material. Therefore, posting a variety of stuff related to your book but not specifically advertising your book can actually increase your chances of being seen. For example, if your book is about the transatlantic railroad, you might include links to scholarly pages about railroads, historical quotes about the railroad, or profiles of famous railroad magnates. It relates to and builds excitement for your topic at the same time.

Before you complete your profile, you'll want to make sure you're prepared to manage each social media account. If you've written a book about microthermal climate regions, for example, and you have no idea how to connect that topic to regular posts on Instagram, perhaps that's not a good fit for you, despite having identified a strong potential audience on that particular platform. This is going to be hard work, but it shouldn't be painfully difficult. Take it one day at a time and pay keen attention to how well your efforts are working.

You'll probably notice words and phrases repeated as hashtags or in descriptions. These are potential keywords, but not always. You want to think of keywords as "stepping stones on the way to finding your book", not "really good terms for describing your book." For example, a slang term used repeatedly on a single Reddit post may not be a great keyword by itself, but if you search all of Reddit for that slang term and come up with a lot of hits relevant to your book or audience—you've found a marketing gold nugget. You can mine all sorts of nuggets just by participating in social media, and it doesn't have to cost a thing.

But not everything is carefree or cost-free. You also want your page to appear in front of your target audience across that social media platform. You will likely have to pay for social media advertisements in

order to broadcast your book's page or author page to a large number
of individuals.

Ads are great in that you don't have to be constantly logged on in
order to get someone's attention. Ads are also annoying, in that you
have to experiment quite a bit before you find something that sticks.
When you're paying for advertising, trial and error can add up quickly,
though social media ads are generally pretty inexpensive and allow you
to set a spending limit.

For most social media platforms, buying ad space guarantees that
your page will be displayed in certain circumstances, to certain users,
with a certain frequency. The more you pay, the more your ad will
appear.

Most social media platforms also allow you to target your ad to the
people most likely to interact with it. Many encourage you to enter
keywords to help limit where your ad is posted. If your book is about
unicorns, it wouldn't make sense to display it to individuals who share
an interest in RV restoration. There might be some overlap in these
categories, but it would be much more worthwhile to spend money
showing people who are interested in mythical creatures or fantasy
characters.

You may be able to enter specific demographic information, such as
age group or where in the world that user might be located. You may
be able to specify personal details about the people who see your ad,
such as gender identity or annual income, depending on which social
media platform you're using.

Your social media ad should be simple, attention-getting, and
memorable. As with your book cover, you want to pay close attention
to the colors, fonts, and pictures you use. It should easily direct users
to your page for more information while making them curious to learn
more. You also need to consider what your ad might look like on

someone's phone screen. A high number of social media users regularly check their accounts via mobile devices, so mobile-compatible formatting is important.

Within the context of social media, you're not just inviting people over to your page to read books with you. You're also becoming a part of the community. You're making others aware of your presence, convincing them that you are the type of person who would write a worthwhile book, and then asking them to give you money for the privilege. You want people to follow you. You want their friends to follow you. You want your page to be suggested. You want as many followers on this free interactive platform as you can muster, all of whom are cheering on your literary success.

Social media can be an amazing way to bolster excitement about your book and gather fans. In most cases, it's free to use, and social media ads are notoriously inexpensive. The downside is that it takes frequent action and interaction in order to establish a reputation, make connections, and rally up a fan base this way.

Websites and Landing Pages

For some authors, social media marketing is enough to help them reach their goals, especially if they've got a large following and great daily interaction. But there are a few reasons why you may want to go further.

As we discussed, those who wish to print a physical paperback and/or hardback version of their book will need to find a way to distribute the copies they sell. Unlike emails, you can't send an actual book immediately, or for free.

One way to distribute your hard copies is to choose a publishing platform that also handles order taking and order fulfillment. The

other option is to create an online location where people can learn
about your book, place an order, and pay you. They should also have
a reasonable expectation that their actions will lead to you shipping
a book to the address they provide. One way to facilitate this sales
process is to create a website.

There are many other benefits to having a website, however. We
just need to refine how we think of a "website." Your book or author
site doesn't need to be a grand affair with loads of sub-pages dedicated
to certain topics or facets of the book. It can be a very simple page
with your author information, a bit of information about the book,
perhaps a few reviews, links to your social media, and a page that allows
them to order their own copy.

To encourage you further, websites are shockingly easy to build in
this day and age. Platforms like WordPress, Squarespace, and Go-
Daddy not only offer users the ability to post a webpage, but include
software that helps you do just that, including help uploading pictures
and videos.

If this is your first time building a website, you might want to
take your time exploring several of the options available to you. You
want to feel comfortable building and updating your site. I encourage
you to enjoy several deep breaths and take advantage of any tutorials or help features offered. The great thing about readily available
website-building platforms is that you can easily find answers to your
questions, contact help staff, or even watch tutorial videos created by
other users on YouTube or social media.

You may choose to add a web design professional to your team as
well, if you are intimidated by the prospect of building your digital
empire by hand. You may also choose to hire a professional if you
want a very good website built very quickly to keep up with an aggressive promotional campaign for your book. As with every other

team member, this will require a significant investment of money and someone else's time. Just because they can build a website in less time than you can doesn't mean they can do it instantly or for free.

Several website-building platforms allow you to integrate a sales feature via a widget or app. Some website building platforms, such as Shopify, are based on selling products. These options might be handy if the only purpose of your website is to facilitate sales.

Which brings up a great question: What kind of goals should you have for your website?

You have the ability to put anything you want on your website. As mentioned before, you should definitely include book information and author information on your website. But there are a few things that you can incorporate as your time, skill, and effort permit. These include:

- **A blog.** Make sure it's relevant to your book or your work as an author. While it's ok to get somewhat personal, this is not the place to analyze your personal life. You might post ruminations about a certain topic in your book, any sources of inspiration, your writing process, or plans for your next book.

- **Excerpts.** A great way to get a reader interested in your material is to give them a small sample of it. On your website, you may wish to post part of your book as an example of what awaits those who buy. As a rule, you don't want to give away all of the details. Instead, consider a page or two that can easily stand alone or could be easily introduced with a little explanation, such as *"Join our heroes Bret and Michael as they enter the enchanted cabin for the first time."* The first chapter is generally a good place to start, but try not to post

more than a few pages for your excerpt. You do want them
to eventually buy the book, after all!

- **Readings**. If you feel comfortable doing so, you may wish
to record audio or video readings of your book. Another
option is to record someone in your target audience reading
your book. This can be heartwarming, such as having a small
child read a picture book, or encouraging, in the case of a
reader sharing an excerpt of a self-help book. You might
even consider a brief animation of your text, even if you
haven't written a picture book. Essentially, you are providing prospective readers with an example of how they might
interact with your book. You want them to feel like they're
reading the book and leave them wanting to read more.

- **Pictures or graphics.** If your book includes some form
of visual, you may wish to include a few samples on your
website. For example, if your book has illustrations of the
characters, you could include character profiles with their
portrait displayed. Always be conscious of what was included in your contract with your visual artist, however. If you
paid for print use only, it's important to make sure they're
ok with their images being displayed in other places. On the
other hand, your contract may stipulate that the images they
create are yours to use anywhere and everywhere. Keep it
legal.

- **Reviews.** With permission, you may wish to post some of
the feedback from your early readers on your website. Most
of us appreciate knowing that what we're about to spend
money on isn't a total waste of our time, so seeing the opin-

ions of others can help drive sales.

- **Keywords.** You have the freedom to put all sorts of keywords in all sorts of places on your website. Throughout the page descriptions. In the photo captions. On your blog. Anywhere you choose to put text on your website, you can put keywords to give your site a chance of showing up when people search for terms related to your book. But again—no keyword stuffing.

You might be wondering, "Can't I put all of this on social media?" The answer is yes, of course you can. And if you have a website, you absolutely should post some of those materials on your social media accounts.

Ultimately, social media posts have a very short life within the algorithm. You might be lucky to appear on your followers' feeds for 24 hours before a new wave of browsing, keywords, and search trends arrives. Yes, people can link to your post and share your post forever (in most cases), but a post usually only appears once on someone's social media feed before it's scrolled past and forgotten forever.

A website is a more permanent fixture. You can plaster a link to your site on anything, from your email signature file to actual stickers that cling to anything (do not deface anything in your pursuit of sales, please). Your site should ultimately serve as a hub for everything related to your book, from what it's about to where one can buy it.

If you're not quite ready for a full website but like the idea of being able to manage distribution online, you might choose to build a simple landing page. A landing page is a single page that requests a single action from those who read it.

I like to think of landing pages as the coupons of the online retail world—you're given a clear action to complete along with a solid understanding of what you'll receive for your efforts. In fact, sometimes landing pages are discount coupons. If you do any shopping online, you've probably encountered those pages that promise 10% off your order if you subscribe to their email list. That's an example of a landing page in prime form. Instead of a discount, however, your readers might enter their email address to receive a downloadable file of your eBook, or click a link to purchase the latest book in your series from Amazon.

Landing pages and websites are not mutually exclusive. In fact, one of my favorite traits about the current generation of technology is how easily we can link one thing to another. You can start with a single social media account, then branch into a few social media accounts, while simultaneously creating a landing page, then eventually build a website, and all of them can cooperate harmoniously by following the instructions for linking and embedding.

Email Campaigns

In fact, one common use for landing pages is to cultivate names and addresses for your email campaign. An email campaign starts by deciding what you want to do with all of the email addresses you gather.

Some authors send out email newsletters announcing new projects, sharing fun facts about their book or topic, or by asking questions to start dialogue, which often flows from email replies to social media comment sections, where people who aren't part of the email catch wind of it, feel left out, and sign up for the next email campaign. Hopefully.

Others sweeten the deal by sending exclusive content to those to subscribe to their email list. This content should be something additional and related to your book, like supplemental text, extra graphics, downloadable activity sheets, or a companion worksheet. You want your audience to want to engage with you, and giving them a little treat for the effort can certainly be endearing.

An email list can also give your readers a way to interact with you directly. Some authors intentionally ask for responses from their readers so they can continue to write content that is meaningful to their audience. Readers often value a connection with an author they admire, though I encourage you to use email management programs such as MailChimp to provide a bit of security from malicious individuals.

The goal is to email your subscribers frequently enough that they remember your name, but not so frequently that they get annoyed and unsubscribe. This tolerance level differs for each individual, but can also be dependent on genre and subject.

So, how do you put all of this together? A lot of it depends on the book you have written. A book about the evolution of synthetic fabrics might only have so much to give in terms of updates and chatter, but provide a parade of interesting Instagram photos or related Pinterest posts. A series about a fictional group of high schoolers might be perfect fodder for a weekly newsletter. In fact, you could potentially create a social media account for each of the characters with a landing page that gathers email addresses for a personalized email from the readers' favorite characters.

But those are just a few examples of how you can use the content of the book you just lovingly wrote and published to promote the book itself. Tools that you can obtain for free on the internet can help inspire an international marketing campaign. You can create whatever digital presence you wish for your own book. You can start and stop at any time, and you have complete control over what you spend—both monetarily and emotionally. That's part of the beauty of self-publishing your book!

Online Ads

We discussed social media ads, but those only appear to potential readers when they're using a particular social media platform.

Online ads are much further ranging—and generally more expensive as a result. For many first-time authors, spending the big bucks right away doesn't necessarily make sense. Many authors don't gain commercial traction until they have several books on the market. A bunch of pricey, splashy, in-your-face ads might make you feel like you've done something important to market your book, but in reality, readers will just see a lot of noise and a single book by an author no one has heard of. Some of them might be curious, but others will be suspicious of all the pomp and circumstance. As much as I hate to say this, physical books have become somewhat of a luxury, and there are quite a few readers who will wait until a new author has more positive reviews and a decent reputation before investing in them. I encourage first-time authors to start with the free and less expensive options before dropping serious amounts.

Some publishing platforms also allow for onsite advertising. Amazon, for example, allows authors who publish through their platform several options for advertising their book, from keyword-triggered sponsored ads to Amazon Author Pages, and limited-time promotions. There are generally fees associated with these activities, and the ads are limited to those who are actively shopping on Amazon. To help contain your spending, you have the ability to control how much is spent by setting a budget and entering the most important keywords that will help users find your book.

Most advertising platforms are set up for "pay-per-click" inter-action, including Google ads and many private websites that accept ads. That typically means that you have to pay for the ad only when individuals click or tap on it. Unfortunately, you have to pay regardless of whether the person doing the clicking meant to or not.

You'll also set a length of time for your ad to run, and create copy for your ad. Unlike social media ads, where you can typically use a photo from your account and enter a quick blurb about why people should follow you, this ad has to stand out from every other character, image, color, and animation relentlessly blasted directly into one's soul as they browse the internet.

Furthermore, when you have an ad, you need it to go somewhere when people click on it. Will it go to your landing page so folks can subscribe to your email newsletter and fun insider exclusives? Will it go to your Amazon Author Page, your website, or Facebook page?

Big decisions must be made when it comes to running internet ads, and I encourage you to research ads thoroughly before you jump into an intense campaign. It's the sort of thing people much wiser than I write entire volumes about. This section is intended as a brief overview of potential opportunities and is no substitute for a solid understanding of how internet ads work. Before you start running ads anywhere, do your research on what methods do and don't work in your niche. "Save your cents for things that make cents" is definitely a valid saying here.

And remember, you can ramp up your advertising efforts at any time, as your budget and personal life allow. Maybe you don't launch a full campaign a week after your book is published, but a year later. We'll talk about planning momentarily.

Giveaways

If your goal is to make money off of your book, giving away copies for free may seem counterintuitive. Why would you want to give away what you intend to sell?

At some point in your life, you have likely heard the words, "You have to go check out this book I just read." You may have uttered these words yourself. Readers enjoy talking about books that they have found useful, entertaining, and informative. When folks are talking about your book, that can lead to higher sales as one person tells another, who tells another, and so on.

But distributing free copies of your book doesn't mean standing on the corner handing out print copies to anyone who will take them. You'll want to be strategic about how you give away your book.

The first line of marketing attack is usually friends and family, as long as they're interested in your particular genre. It's not fair to ask anyone to struggle through a book that means nothing to them when they could be reading one of the billions of other options in this world.

Instead, choose people who would want to read your book even if you didn't write it. These individuals have the highest chance of not only enjoying your book but also recommending it to others who share their reading preferences. They might add it to the must-read list for their book club, share their feelings about it on their social media pages, or otherwise spread the word about your book, thus increasing sales without anyone spending a penny.

You may also wish to explore literary feedback platforms such as Goodreads or Booksprout. Through these sites, you may allow readers to request a copy of your book, which you'll deliver to them digitally, free of charge. These readers will then review your book. Most of the time, these reviews are not considered private and can be published not just on that platform, but on your website, sales page, social media, or Amazon Author Page.

This can also provide greater traction for book sales. People want to know what they're getting into before they put their precious time and money into your book, and reading positive reviews from real readers can help them feel more confident in clicking that "Place Order" button. The more evidence they have assuring them that your book is a good and worthy read, the more likely they are to take the plunge themselves.

You can also run contests on social media, allowing a small number of lucky individuals a free advance copy of your book. In general, people love free stuff. They also love winning. Your contest can be simple, such as "One lucky reader will be able to read my book tonight—comment on this post for a chance to win a free advance copy of (Title)!" You might also have contests that encourage engagement, such as "Tag 3 friends and all of you get a copy of my book for free!"

Ultimately, you don't want to give your book away for free to anyone who bats their eyelashes and says "pretty please," but you can give your book a substantial nudge towards more sales by giving free copies to the right people. So it might be ok to give a few to the "pretty please" crowd, but ask for reviews or recommendations in return. Not every casual reader may oblige with that part, but hopefully, they'll at least tell someone about how much they enjoyed your book.

Guest Appearances

Don't get too excited—this is not your network television talk show debut. Instead, you'll be looking for opportunities to present yourself and your work to someone else's audience.

Naturally, you can't just barge into the comment section of a stranger's social media page or website with your stunning essay about whatever you felt like writing that morning. Instead, this process needs to be strategic.

As you scour forums, fan groups, and social media pages, you'll likely connect with others who are trying to make their way in the literary world or who specialize in your topic. They may have their own blogs, websites, YouTube channels, podcasts, or other outlets where they share their own work. And they might also be willing to let you make a guest appearance.

You may wish to reach out to those you already follow and admire. Briefly explain who you are if you aren't already acquainted, and ask if they accept guest postings. Be upfront about the fact that you've just published a book, and you think it would be a great fit for their community. They might ignore your request, or say no, but there's always the chance they'll agree that you would make a fantastic guest on their platform.

Once everyone has agreed, you'll want to be prepared for what your guest appearance will entail. For a video or podcast, you might be asked to be part of a panel or co-host an episode. If you're asked to make a guest post on a website or blog, you'll be asked to stay on a particular topic or ruminate on a certain subject so that your post doesn't derail your host's own self-promotion.

You'll likely be able to share some information about your book, but you won't be the primary focus. Don't be dissuaded if your book promotion is limited to a quick blurb at the end. You're a guest. You shouldn't expect to put your shoes on the furniture, so to speak. This is your host's livelihood, so act appropriately. Don't try to hijack their platform, oversell yourself, or distract from their regular business. Do communicate with your host ahead of time so you're aware of your roles and responsibilities as a guest.

Selling your self-published book is not a bloodsport—it's an exercise in finding your place in a very big world where every potential opportunity counts. Participating in your niche's community through guest blogs or guest appearances is an excellent way for readers to connect with you as a person and through your books.

Evaluating Costs and Expenses

The two biggest commitments to executing a marketing plan for your book are time and money, with time being the most consequential.

You can do a lot of marketing for free. You can set up social media accounts for free. You can build a website or landing page for free. But you're still going to need the time to make it happen.

Gaining social media momentum takes a lot of strategic work. First, you have to find your audience. Then you need to interact with them. You need to learn when they do most of their social media browsing so you can pop up at the right time on their feed. You need to carefully build a community. All of this takes time, but you can do it without entering your credit card number anywhere.

Likewise, maintaining an email campaign requires plenty of effort. You'll need to establish an email address for yourself, gather email addresses, come up with and write content for regular emails to your subscribers, decide how often to send these emails to them, and respond to any replies within a reasonable amount of time.

Building a website also takes time. Yes, drag-and-drop technology has made it easier than ever to create each page of your site to your specifications, but it still takes time. Plus, you'll need to keep up with site maintenance. Sometimes links break. Sometimes photos won't load. Sometimes an entire hosting site goes down for days. While a website doesn't require the daily attention a social media account does, you'll still need to keep an eye on it.

All of this requires an incredible amount of organization, in that you'll need to keep track of how things are going on each particular channel of your marketing campaign. This includes, but is certainly not limited to:

- What did you reply to which user on which platform

- Which posts are receiving more attention and why

- Who is actually opening your emails, and are they reading them

- How many followers are engaging with your posts through each channel

- How many followers are engaging on multiple channels (Facebook and X, for example)

Thankfully, we live in an age where online entrepreneurs are common. As a result, there are plenty of programs that can help you recognize, organize, and balance all of these spinning plates. You'll find examples and websites for these programs in the Resources section, of course, but let's look at a few common options. Your interest in each option will depend on your goals and the intensity of your campaign.

- **Content marketing sites** provide you with tools to build ads and visuals relating to your book. You can create landing pages, fancy graphics, logos, letterhead, email templates, advertisements, and more here, all of which can be loaded to your website or social media platforms.

- **Analytics and digital marketing tools** can help you understand where your advertising money is going, how people are interacting with your material, allow you to run side-by-side comparison campaigns, and even help you capture demographic information about those who like, follow, and subscribe to all of your different platforms.

- **Email marketing sites** help you manage incoming and outgoing emails, including newsletters. These platforms allow you to store the email addresses of your subscribers as well as help you analyze how people are interacting with your emails. Best of all, you can schedule future emails in batches, so that a certain group of subscribers will receive Email A on Tuesday at 10am, while another group receives Email B on Wednesday at 5pm, as an example.

- **Social media management sites** allow you to schedule content across social media channels. You can often upload images or written content for an entire campaign, create a calendar, and your posts will be generated as you wish. Instead of making sure you're sitting in front of your computer at the perfect time, these tools will post according to your schedule.

Such tools also allow you analytical insight into your social media posts and ads. They can track the performance of everything you do on social media, as well as everything others do to interact with your social media platforms.

These sites and the tools they provide frequently require some form of subscription or membership to utilize all of the features. Some will provide a free version, but that version is always somewhat limited. The good news is that, unless you're planning an aggressive campaign, the free version is often a fine place to get started, and upgrades can often be purchased at any time.

Whether you choose to include software and tools in your marketing plan or have another type of organization plan in mind, I encourage you to take things one day, one post, and one channel at a time. It's all too easy to get disoriented online. Maybe Taylor3_75 liked your book on Instagram, but Taylor735 left a scathing reply to your last Reddit comment. You don't want to get these two individuals confused when responding to their insights.

So now that you know what you can do and how you can do it, I suggest you come up with a plan to help you find the right path through the chaos.

Coming Up with a Realistic Marketing Plan

It feels like we've gotten very far away from the part where we wrote a book, doesn't it? This step has been so full of keywords and strategy that you might have lost sight of what we were doing in the first place. The truth is that it's very easy to get swept away by the myriad possibilities for marketing your book, especially when this isn't your full-time job.

Therefore, I encourage every writer to come up with a realistic plan before they launch a campaign for their book.

The first thing you need to decide is "What is success?" We talked about this earlier, in a broader sense of knowing what your goals are for your book. In the case of your marketing plan, you've got to look more at the trees than the forest as a whole.

Each time you interact with someone from your author account on social media, you're running a microscopic marketing campaign. Most of the time, these interactions have a neutral impact as just another post or comment on the World Wide Web. But after a while, other users of that platform will start associating your user name with your voice. You'll become a member of the community. People will want to associate with you and learn more about you, including what lovely books you've published recently. Everything you do to promote yourself as an author or your book as its own entity has an impact.

Subsequently, "success" can be measured by many things, from the number of likes your comments and posts get to the number of people who click on your link and actually purchase your book (we call those "conversions," by the way).

So let's get organized. If you're at a loss for how to get started, here's a little cheat sheet I came up with years ago, before I was able to invest in programs that could help me track all of this without notes. I still use it frequently, if not in full format, in practice any time I'm interacting online on behalf of my books.

And as with any of my exercises or worksheets, I encourage you to embrace the concept and make it your own. You can add or subtract fields to meet your individual needs.

For this example, I'm pretending to market the zebra-orphan space buddy book from earlier. It's a dystopian science fiction book for teenagers (BISAC *JUV053000 JUVENILE FICTION/Science Fiction*

/ General and *JUV059000 JUVENILE FICTION / Dystopian*) with several black-and-white sketch-style illustrations.

Goal	100 new followers on the book's Facebook page
Timeline	30 days
Start Date	1 May
End Date	30 May
Budget	$0
How Will I Define Success?	1. When I receive 100 new followers 2. Especially if I can do it within one month 3. No ads- all organic
Steps I Will Take to Reach My Goal	1. Interact in at least 2 social media posts daily 2. Join one new group each week 3. Start a new discussion on (Group) 4. Post for feedback in (Forum) 5. Run a contest in which members tag three additional friends to win a free mini cookbook of recipes from the zebra's home planet.

You can even drill down further into your steps by creating plans for each of them, as well.

Goal	Run a contest in which members tag three additional friends to win a free mini cookbook of recipes from the zebra's home planet.
Timeline	30 days
Start Date	1 May
End Date	30 May
Budget	$0
How Will I Define Success?	When people start tagging others on my post
Steps I Will Take to Reach My Goal	1. Announce contest on all social media channels 2. Write and edit the mini-cookbook 3. Boost contest weekly on all social media channels 4. Contact (Groups) to see if I can announce my contest on their social media channels 5. Daily reminders in the final week 6. Compile entries 7. Choose winner 8. Send them the mini-cookbook as a PDF

It's not a profound document, but it's enough to ensure I don't lose sight of three very important things:

- What is success?

- How much time and effort can I give it?

- How much money will I spend towards making success happen?

I've somewhat alluded to it throughout this step, but it needs to be said straightforwardly: your marketing efforts will likely change over time.

Not all of the plans you create will be successful. You might find yourself at the end of May with 50 likes. That doesn't mean it was a bad plan. It just means you need to make a new plan.

The thing about marketing is that sometimes it fails even when it shouldn't.

Once upon a time, I fell in love with a particular garlic crust at my local pizza place. I couldn't get enough of it. I found excuses to order garlic crust pizza every chance I got. Friends coming over? Garlic crust. Brother got accepted to college? Garlic crust. It's Tuesday? Garlic crust.

Every time I got it, though, people acted as though I plucked this particular treat from the ether. "You got this from that place? I didn't even know they had this!" they would enthuse.

It wasn't that I ordered from a secret menu; it's just that these folks hadn't stumbled across the same Instagram post I had, where someone does a long, juicy, drool-worthy slow-motion cheese pull with a giant slice of garlic crust pizza. I, on the other hand, had seen this post during the afternoon while bored and counting down the hours until dinner. I was just the right person seeing just the right post at just the right time. It made a huge impact on me, while my loved ones and associates had missed it completely.

Such is the reality of digital marketing. You can do your absolute textbook best, and still not get the textbook results you hoped for. At the same time, you have to appreciate whatever wins you get. Even though I was the only person who saw the Instagram post, I made at least a dozen people aware of the delicious garlic crust pizza. I know for a fact that some of those individuals are ordering garlic crust pizza to this day.

I'm certainly not going to dissuade you from setting big overall goals for your book, but I will caution you to go slow. Adjust your stride as you are able. Little steps can net big results while huge efforts can fizzle like fireworks in the rain.

Above all, do not burn out. This is your book that you published. It is truly a life-altering experience to publish a book, and it is even possible for it to be an overall positive life-altering experience. You can start and stop your marketing efforts whenever you want. Nothing is required, nothing is guaranteed, and all any of us can do is our very best.

And what should you do when sales have slumped and updating your social media channels feels like screaming into the void?

It's obvious, isn't it? You write another book and do it all over again. "From the author of (Your First Book) comes a new installment, (Your Second Book)!"

Chapter Six

How to Survive the Publication of Your Own Book

R emember way back at the beginning of this book, when you were writing or had just finished writing a book? We've talked about a lot of things since then. It may feel like your manuscript has faded away in the rearview mirror as we've zipped quickly through publishing methods and the wild world of marketing.

It is a lot to take in, and we moved quickly through a variety of topics. I hope you take the time to dig deeper, not just with the resources I've included, but on your own. This is your book and your experience. I've given you a basic outline of some of the most popular tools to consider on your journey, but don't feel like you are required to do any of these things.

I once had a friend who self-published a book. He didn't have much interest in digital marketing, but he has a lot of friends. He threw a massive party to celebrate—his neighbors even got involved with the hullabaloo. Like I said, he's very charming and people like him. His book was a murder mystery set in the 1920s. He recruited some of his close friends to dress up and act like characters from his book. Guests and neighbors were encouraged to wear period costumes as well. I'm not sure how many copies my friend sold that night or ever, but it certainly was a memorable way to spread the word about his book. If I'm talking about it years later, I'm sure other attendees do as well.

My point is that the self-publication and promotion of your first book shouldn't consume your every thought, cause you untold agony, or require major alterations in your lifestyle.

The simplest piece of advice I can give you is "Don't be in a rush." That's it. Be pragmatic. Be careful. And even if it seems like I went way overboard with all of the research and pre-work, please know that I did so for a reason. It is impossible to be over-prepared for the self-publication process.

Therefore, I'll leave you with the three concepts that help keep me sane and headed in the right direction through the self-publishing process. Whether or not my lists and worksheets are ideal for you, I consider this the triumvirate of tenets for self-publishing sanity.

Identify Your Goals. I know I've said this many times, but the best way to stay focused on the process at hand is to know what you're trying to accomplish and why.

Many of us identify big goals first. "I want to sell my book" is an example of a great big nebulous goal. This is a great place to start, but then ask yourself, "how?" and "why?" Keep asking yourself these questions until you find a simple action that you can do today. Take notes along the way so you can remember some of the great ideas you came up with along the way, too. I keep a notebook on my desk just for such brain wanderings, and it's saved me from forgetting a lot of great goals and ideas on how to reach them.

Stay Organized. I can't emphasize this part enough, either. You'll want to have a clear idea of what you're supposed to be doing as you plan for each goal. It is far too easy to start many metaphorical fires, only to forget which ones are burning.

Consider keeping a record of each action you take, no matter how small and inconsequential it may seem at the time. I've had what I thought was an offhand comment on social media gain far more attention than I expected—if you know where and when you made that comment, you can gain some insight into hot topics and what your audience is interested in, right now.

This is also true when managing your team. You'll want to keep track of who has your book and when you should expect them to complete their work on it. You'll want to keep track of who gets paid what and when, and contact information for your team members.

I've included a few sample worksheets in the Resources section to help you get an idea of how to get your record-keeping and organization started. Some of the tools we discussed include tools like this, but before you invest in those tools, I encourage you to get a feel for what information you'll want to track and how. Make this process your own!

Maintain Your Budget. Yes, this is technically part of the "stay organized" concept, but it is important enough to warrant its own bullet point. It is tragically easy to lose sight of who gets paid what and when, especially when you're trying to get your book uploaded, setting up accounts on social media, and trying to gain a community, researching keywords, and considering what other team members you need. No one likes a delayed payday, no matter how understanding they are of the reasons behind it.

Even if you're financially solvent to the point where money is no issue, this can also be a helpful reminder of exactly how much you've sunk into your book at any given point. As a first-time self-publisher, you may want to keep costs to a minimum until you know for a fact that you can get a return on your investment.

Of course there are plenty of other practical considerations, such as getting the right amount of sleep for you, drinking plenty of water, and letting yourself take plenty of breaks away from your computer screen, desk, office, house, neighborhood... whatever it takes to keep your book stress at a reasonable level. Go slow, and keep it positive.

Conclusion

If, upon reading this, you're thinking, "I'm not doing all of that," I encourage you to follow through with that plan.

Self-publishing a book can be a serious commitment, but exactly how momentous this process becomes is entirely up to you.

Write a book. Write the book you want to write, the way you want to write it. If you want to sell lots of copies, try some of the suggestions I've recommended. If you don't want to sell lots of copies, your participation is entirely voluntary.

Make that book the best version it can be. Involve other people in the success of your book. Much like a parent tuning out a crying child in the supermarket, we can often miss our own mistakes. It's a great idea to have more sets of eyes on your book to help you see those oversights. And of course, you don't have to take all of their suggestions, after all. Maybe you should take their word for it on typos, though, at the bare minimum.

Publish your book. There are many publication paths to ponder, from the traditional agent/publisher relationship to self-publishing. While I've given you some things to consider about each option, remember my list isn't exhaustive, and there are plenty of ins and outs that are specific to certain types of books or publishing houses.

If you do self-publish your book, choose your publishing platform carefully, based on your needs. Do you want built-in advertising and distribution services? How compatible are you with the process of uploading your book to that platform? How easy is formatting?

For marketing your book—well, I've given you a few examples to get your idea machine started, but there really is no limit to what you can do to persuade other people to buy your book. Your imagination—and persistence—is the most important part.

In fact, there's really no limit at all to what you can do with your self-published book. While it's less likely that your self-published book series will be turned into a major motion picture franchise within a year of release, it isn't unheard of to start soliciting screenplay writers and producers to consider your book as their next project. But that process is its own book entirely.

As a final note, I'd like to wish you the best on your self-publishing journey. I hope this book has opened your eyes to what the process of self-publishing your book can entail. I hope you choose your own path wisely, and though things might not go exactly as you planned, I hope these become learning moments that lead to a brighter future.

Now go write a book—I can't wait to read it!

Resources

A s promised, here is a compilation of resources to help you get started on your own self-publishing journey.

I encourage you to treat this list as a starting place, rather than an exhaustive collection—remember, this is your book, and you're allowed to pursue other sites, sources, and opportunities that make sense for your book. I've arranged them to correlate with the section of the book that mentions these resources.

As always, I need to remind you that I have no affiliation with any of these sites. I'm not a sponsor, these aren't affiliate links, and no one profits from the sharing of this information but you. Use it in good health!

Information Gathering

In this section, I mentioned resources for connecting with the literary community and discovering where people talk about books. Here are just a few sites, but remember, you can also start with Facebook groups, Reddit communities, or by gathering a few friends in your living room!

Scribophile: https://www.scribophile.com/

Shut Up & Write: https://www.shutupwrite.com/

Writer's Cafe: https://www.writerscafe.org/

Writers Helping Writers: https://writershelpingwriters.net/

Note that many of these sites have forums specifically designed to connect you with beta readers, editors, and other potential team members, as well.

Hiring a Team

Finding editors, beta readers, designers, formatters, artists, marketing help, or web design can be a chore, especially if you've never hired someone before. Here are some resources to help you find talent and know what you should pay them.

Editorial Freelancers Association : https://www.the-efa.org/

LinkedIn: https://www.linkedin.com/

Upwork: https://www.upwork.com/

Fiverr: https://www.fiverr.com/

Interview Worksheet

This is a basic template I use when reaching out to prospective team members. These questions help me understand how a potential collaboration might work, while the checklist helps me gauge if the partnership is really what I'm looking for.

Questions:

- Why are you interested in this project?

- Tell me a bit about other projects you've worked on. What were you able to accomplish for that author?

- What skills make you a good fit for this project?

- What sort of timeline would you anticipate for my project?

- If you were to win this role, how would you get started?

Checklist

- Do they respond to communication quickly? Thoroughly?

- Do they seem interested in the project?

- Do you feel confident that their pricing structure is appropriate for the job

- Have they provided samples of their work?

- Are they upfront with their plans, prices, and skill level?

Pay careful attention to not only the contents of the messages they send to you, but also when they send them, and how thoroughly they answer your questions. When I was getting started long ago, I remember being shocked when I received replies to my inquiries, despite having a very slim portfolio of mostly collegiate efforts. I've got a few of these clients to this day, and I asked one of them why he chose me when he could see I was brand new to the industry. "Because the email you sent me made sense, answered all of my questions, was grammatically correct, and didn't annoy me," he replied. I encourage you to hold your team members to this standard, as well.

Keep It Legal

Say it again: "We do not plagiarize." Check out these sources for information on how to keep yourself from accidentally committing a crime—literary or Federal.

Examples of different types of formatting and citation:

https://pitt.libguides.com/citationhelp

https://www.grammarly.com/blog/academic-writing/format-a-research/

https://kindlepreneur.com/how-to-format-a-book/

Copyright Law:

https://www.copyright.gov/engage/writers/

https://copyrightalliance.org/education/industry/writers/

https://www.copyright.gov/what-is-copyright/

Use of Images Laws: https://www.copyrightlaws.com/legally-using-images/

Public Domain for fiction and non-fiction writers:

https://www.copyright.gov/fair-use/

https://www.copyrightlaws.com/copyright-laws-in-u-s-government-works/

How to Query

Traditional publishing and self-publishing are not mutually exclusive! If you decide to go this route or want to explore possibilities, here are a few places to start.

Publishers Marketplace: https://www.publishersmarketplace.com/

QueryTracker: https://querytracker.net/

Duotrope: https://duotrope.com/

Association of American Literary Agents (AALA): https://aalitagents.org/

Self-Publishing Platforms

This list is not exhaustive or evergreen, but a good place to get started!

Amazon KDP: https://kdp.amazon.com/en_US/

Barnes & Noble Press: https://press.barnesandnoble.com/

IngramSpark: https://www.ingramspark.com/

Apple Books: https://www.apple.com/apple-books/

Kobo: https://www.kobo.com/

Draft2Digital: https://www.draft2digital.com/

Lulu: https://www.lulu.com/

Thankfully, it's easy and free for anyone to read about these important parts of self-publishing.

ISBN: https://www.isbn.org/

BISAC: https://www.bisg.org/complete-bisac-subject-headings-list

Marketing Resources

I threw out a lot of unfamiliar terms and quick explanations in this step. The good news is that there are plenty of opportunities to learn more, along with platforms and programs that can help you keep up with all of the options available to you.

Content management

Contentful: https://www.contentful.com/

Adobe Experience Manager: https://business.adobe.com/products/experience-manager/adobe-experience-manager.html

Analytic tools

Google Analytics: https://marketingplatform.google.com/about/analytics/

Semrush: https://www.semrush.com/

Email campaign management

Mail Chimp: www.mailchimp.com

Adobe Campaign: https://business.adobe.com/products/campaign/email-marketing.html

Social media management

Hootsuite: www.hootsuite.com

Loomly: www.loomly.com

Web advertising
Google Ad Manager: https://admanager.google.com/home/
OpenX: https://www.openx.com/

Website building
WordPress: https://wordpress.com/
Wix: https://www.wix.com/
Shopify: www.shopify.com
Squarespace: www.squarespace.com
General Marketing Assistance
Hubspot Academy: https://academy.hubspot.com/
Ahrefs Academy: https://ahrefs.com/academy
Search   Engine   Land   Marketing   101:
https://searchengineland.com/guide/marketing-101

Book Giveaway Sites
GoodReads: https://www.goodreads.com/author/program
Library Thing: https://www.librarything.com/ner/howitworksof-ferer

Organization Worksheets

Again, these are not super-formal worksheets, but merely options to get you started as you progress through the self-publishing process. I've added a few examples so you can get a feel for how I use these tools.

Time Tracking

Action	Steps	Started (time, day)	Due (time, day)	Ended (time, date)	Results	Next Steps
Make Instagram Account	• Create user name • Upload profile pictures • Create first six posts	21, May 2:25am	22, May 4:40pm	21, May 6:52am	All steps complete	• Follow other accounts • Announce Instagram account on other channels • Schedule first post
Edit book	• Send to Editors A, B, C • Resolve edits • Review edits • Make necessary changes	Sent to Editor A June 1; Sent to Editors B and C June 3	All editors have a due date of June 21	Ongoing	Ongoing	Send to beta readers after Round 1 of editing; Send to formatting after final edits

Expense Tracking

Action	Cost	Due Date/Duration	Results
Hire web designer	$100/hour	Deadline 7/29 Projected 4 hours	(Ongoing)
Facebook ad	$1/day	30 days	4 new follows 12 new comments 30 shares

5 Writing Exercises

If you're interested in learning to write books, chances are high that you've tried before and gotten stuck. As a result, you may be even less enthusiastic about trying again. If that's the case, check out some personally selected writing exercises from author Lauren Bingham's vault of helpful tricks and tips for getting the cursor moving again... or for the first time. Go to https://subscribepage.io/5-Writing-Exercises to download your own copy of Lauren Bingham's Five Favorite Writing Exercises.

About the author

Lauren Bingham grew up in a house full of books. A dedicated bibliophile by first grade, she often got into trouble for voraciously consuming any written material—from consuming Reader's Digest cover to cover in one sitting to completing library books before they even made it home.

Lauren has been avidly writing for pure passion since childhood, and thanks to the internet for providing a comfortable place where all writers are welcome. Ghostwriting and copywriting since the early 2000s, she believes strongly that there is a story in each of us and that any time is a great time to share those stories with others.

Reviews and feedback help improve this book and the author. If you enjoy this book, we would greatly appreciate it if you could take a few moments to share your opinion and post a review on Amazon. Thank you!

Also by Lauren Bingham

www.ingramcontent.com/pod-product-compliance
Lightning Source LLC
Chambersburg PA
CBHW070125030426
42335CB00016B/2267